T0380285

White Lies

Ginamarie Foceri

BALBOA.PRESS
A DIVISION OF HAY HOUSE

Cover Art Credit: Stefania Zimmerman

Balboa Press books may be ordered through booksellers or by contacting:

Balboa Press
A Division of Hay House
1663 Liberty Drive
Bloomington, IN 47403
www.balboapress.com
1 (877) 407-4847

Print information available on the last page.

ISBN: 978-1-9822-4690-7 (sc)
ISBN: 978-1-9822-4689-1 (e)

Balboa Press rev. date: 05/15/2020

I dedicate this book to:

My family for their love and support.

To Dexter R. Allen and Alex Cozier Barber for putting this idea in my head on my 18th birthday; To all my girls, this is to you. You all in some way or form inspired me and I thank you for that.

My bestie Delveter Casper, for 20 years, it has been nothing but love, guidance and true friendship without expectation or judgment. Love you.

Benjamin "BigFace Bennie" Malave and Mike "M.I. Nyce" San Inocencio - You guys made me pick up my pen again. Much love and always respect!!!

Lauren Schechter for editing this book for me and Stefania Zimmerman for the cover art.

Chapter 1

When her cell phone starts to glow a bright pink light, and howl to the tune of best friends by 50 Cent and Olivia, Aubrielle Miakova's heart begins to race. As she reaches to answer it, already knowing that it is Chance on the other end, she wonders why her heart still speeds up when he calls; Was it because she still loved him, or because she knows what lies ahead.

Chance's real name is James Curtis. Everyone refers to him as Chance because he gets away with too many encounters with either the ladies or the law. He is very handsome by all accounts. His perfect body stands at 6 feet 2 inches, weighing in at 186 pounds, and every bit of it being muscle. His skin is as smooth as a newborn and the same color as Nesquik. He always has a fresh Caesar cut, as he is at the barber shop often for an edge up and a shave. Who knew hair grew that fast? His outfit and sneakers were just right. They had to be fresh crisp and clean always, but what really gets him all the attention are his emerald green eyes. He grew up on the streets of Long Island, New York. No family to speak of, an only child who never knew his father. It was just Chance and his mother, Joanna, his whole life. They were extremely close and did everything together. Joanna used to tell everyone that Chance was the apple of her eye. They had an amazing mother-son bond and were even best friends. Chance told her everything. There was nothing they wouldn't do for each other, which was made clear when Joanna took a bullet to protect him.

It was one hot summer day. Chance was about 6 years old when he was outside riding his bike with a group of kids. When the couple next door to them began to fight, Violet came home from work early and caught Corey having sex with one of his side chicks. Tired of all he put her through, Violet began to shoot her 9mm gun at both him and the girl. Even after they tried to flee the apartment, she followed them out to the streets where the kids were playing and left vulnerable. Joana heard the commotion and ran outside after Chance, throwing her body over him and the other children to shield them so they would not get hit by any of the bullets. Joanna was hit three times. She was a hero to everyone where they lived, until she was murdered on Chance's 18th birthday in the housing complex where they lived.

Homestead was known for drugs, murder, robberies, and pretty much any other crime known to man; not to mention its glooming and depressingly ugly appearance. The buildings were all brown with bricks, they had no grass just dirt, and a dark cloud always seems to hover over it. It was a dead-end apartment complex with lots of speed bumps and no reason to be there unless you were buying drugs, or you had to live there. Homestead was also within a half mile to the closest police station. A toy cop was at the front gate to monitor the activity standing less than 50 feet away, however, nothing was ever done about it anyway. Oh, and let's not forget the funeral home directly across the street, which came in handy from all the murders that took place in Homestead and the surrounding streets.

After the death of his mother, Chance's game was off. He had been hustling for a few years and was smart about his game. He did things in a certain manner, so as not to get caught. He would never sell drugs to anyone that was referred to him by another customer; he would never sell at the same spot twice; he would also never sell to someone if they had another person with them that he didn't know. These were just a few things he did to watch out for himself, but no one ever really knew his rules because they changed daily, or according to the situation. The only rule for sure was Chance always followed his gut feeling, but after his mother's death he did everything backward; it was like he just stopped caring or gave up. Eventually, his mistakes were seen by everyone, including the police.

The police began to follow him, taking note of everything he did. They did not want Chance; they wanted the person who Chance worked for. They figured the best way to get to Izzy was through Chance, or one of his other Distributors, whoever fucked up first. After about a week, they found the break they were looking for. They followed Chance to one of his client's house, Missy's house.

Missy was a 45-year-old crackhead. She had been smoking since she was 12 years old and became a prostitute by the age of 15. Everyone knew her and that she was on parole for life due to a robbery gone bad where an undercover cop was killed in the line of duty. The cop was acting like one of Izzy's distributors to gain information on him and build a case against him. Missy knew him as a dealer and told her friend that they should rob him since he always had piles of cash on him. Even though she wasn't there during the actual robbery, and even though she didn't pull the trigger herself, she was still sentenced to 15 years to life for the murder. She served 12 years and 8 months at Rikers Island correctional facility and released on parole for the rest of her sentence, which was life because she arranges the robbery.

The day after the police saw Chance go to Missy's, her parole officer did an at home pop in visit. The police knew if they gave her a drug test that she would come back dirty because they knew she bought drugs from chance last night. So, after she came back positive for the drugs in her system, they made a deal with her to set up Chance or she would go back to jail and max out their; which meant she would be there for the rest of her life.

Missy introduced Chance to her "friend" who was really a cop, but she told Chance that her friend was also a fen. Chance should have known better than to sell to Missy's friend, Danielle. He always avoided selling to people who referred him to someone like Missy did, in fear of being set up. This was one of the oldest stories in the book, plus Danielle did not have the typical markings of someone on drugs. The only thing Chance really noticed about her, which scared him, was that she was a white woman who was determined to be ghetto no matter the cost; for a Latino or black man it could be deadly. However, he went against everything and sold to her anyway. They watched him for 3 months and after a few sales, tape conversations, and phone calls they had a warrant. To serve the warrant, they had Danielle call him to set up another sale; it was at a local shopping center. Chance was sitting in his rental car, a Lincoln Navigator, waiting on Danielle when he got a bad feeling. He decided to leave since he had been waiting for 20 minutes. He started to pull off when he noticed cop cars coming into the complex from every direction. Chance hit the gas pedal and went to the one opening where he didn't see police cars coming in. As he made it to the opening, he tried to make a sharp left-hand turn which made him lose control of the truck. He went flying across the street on the neighbor's property and crashed into their fence. Chance continued to try to make a getaway and stomped on the gas pedal harder, but because the grass was so soft from all the recent rain the truck barely moved; so he pushed harder this time making the truck move with such force that he drove into a tree. The cops pulled Chance out of the totaled truck and arrested him.

He got 3-6 years for possession, intent to sell, criminal sale of narcotics, and paraphilia. Chance only served 3 years 8 months and 5 days in jail; he was then released on good behavior but was placed on parole for the rest of his sentence.

When he came home it was the spring of 2005. This was the spring he meets Aubrielle, and their lives were never the same again. It was one hot day in late May, and Chance was leaving the gym. As he walked across the street to his car, which was in front of the park, he saw Aubrielle. The first-time chance saw Aubrielle he fell in love with her. Aubrielle looked like she was white, which she got from her mother's side, but her father was Spanish and middle eastern. Aubrielle was a girl with no self-worth. With very low self-esteem, she thought of herself as ugly, and fat, and no one would ever want her. However, there was something very different about Aubrielle which everyone saw the moment they laid eyes on her. She was average yet still very pretty in her own right. She stood at 5 feet 4 inches tall, she was thick and had curves right where they needed to be. She had long honey blonde hair that waterfall to her waistline, with eyes that are bluer than the sky. But it wasn't her physical appearance that made Aubrielle stand out from the rest of them; it was her presence.

While Chance watched her from afar, he tried so hard to figure out what was it about her. Was it her skin that had a soft glow to it, or the way her hair was blowing in the wind; maybe it was the way she helped a little girl that looked to be about 4 years old? The little girl had stepped on a piece of glass, she won't let anyone near her, not any of the other kids or the adult. She kept screaming and reached out in Aubrielle

5

direction. Aubrielle took her from the other lady that was there, they looked like they could be related, Chance thought to himself, as he hopes Giana was the other lady's daughter and not Aubrielle. Once in her arms, Aubrielle wiped away the tears that were swimming down Giana's face.

"Giana close your eyes and count to five with me." Aubrielle directs her.

"No, it's going to hurt." Giana whines.

"No, I'm not going to touch it, just trust me ok?" Aubrielle says sweetly, as Giana nods yes.

When Giana and Aubrielle get three, Aubrielle pulls the piece of glass out of her foot. Giana had no idea until she got to five and opened her eyes to see Aubrielle was holding the piece of glass. She cleaned up her wound and put a bandage on it. The little girl kissed Aubrielle check and then jumped down from the table to go back to the game the other kids were playing. When Giana got halfway back to the kids, she turns a screamed: "thank you aunt brie." "You're welcome, sweetie. Put your shoes back on now." Aubrielle answered her. Giana nodded as she did what she was told.

As chance began to walk over to her, he heard the exchange and was relieved. Chance told her "Hello, that was amazing. Will you have dinner with me sometime?" He asks her. "No, thank you." Aubrielle declines and walks over to her niece to help tie her sneakers she just put back on. As she walks away, she tries to figure out why she just said no, or better yet why did he even ask her at all.

Aubrielle's sister, Anelise, was there when the exchange between Chance and Aubrielle took place. When Aubrielle walks away, Anelise approaches Chance. As she walks over to him "Hey, wait a second." Anelise tells Chance in a voice only loud enough from him to her, she pulls out a random business card from her packet and a pen and writes down Aubrielle information. "Here is my sister name, which is Aubrielle, and her cell phone number," Anelise tells him. "Hey, good looking out – that was amazing; what she did for that little girl. Is that your daughter?"

"Yes, she is. Giana and Aubrielle have a great bond. Aubrielle is a nurse at St. John's Hospital. So, when it comes to bumps, bruises, and being sick, Giana goes to her. She thinks I don't know anything. "Anelise says laughing.

"Well, I better get over there." Anelise continues, as she watches her sister teaching her daughter to tie her shoes. Giana is at the age she wants to learn everything and do everything for herself.

"Well, thank you again for looking out. I'm sorry, what your name is?" Chance asks. "Anelise" she replies. "Well thank you again Anelise, this will come in handy." As he turns and walks away from Anelise, Aubrielle turns around to look for her sister, who is now walking over to her. They watch the kids play and never talk about what happened with Chance. Anelise knows she's not going to talk about it, and it's not over, so she will sit back and wait to see how this plays out.

Later that night Chance calls Aubrielle's cell phone, but it goes straight to voicemail. He chooses not to leave a voice message because he wants to persuade her to go out with him and feels catching her off guard will be better-done face to face; especially since she doesn't even know he has her number. The next morning Chance tries her cell again, and again it goes to her voicemail. However, this time he thinks that she may be at work and remembers that Anelise said she worked at the hospital, so he calls information for the number and then calls her again.

"Hello, St. John's emergency room," Aubrielle says.

"Hello, I'm looking for Aubrielle" Chance states.

Aubrielle is confused, she thinks the voice sounds familiar but cannot place it. It isn't a personal call because only her family had her work number and wouldn't dare call unless it was really an emergency. They knew as a Registered Nurse in a hospital how busy she was, and even on the floor, the non-emergency things were usually very chaotic.

"May, I ask who is calling?" she says. She is trying to get more information without giving herself away.

"Yes, I have a delivery for her. It is our procedure to make sure the person is there to receive it. So, is she there or will she be today?" Chance pries.

"But I'm not expecting anything." she blurts out before realizing it.

"Sometimes, that is half the fun. I will be there shortly." Chance says before he hangs up.

It was now 2:15 pm. Chance thought that she should be getting off shortly, thinking back to how his mother worked 7 am to 3 pm as a nurse. She may have had to come in early or stay late but that is a bridge he will cross when he gets to it. Chance takes a quick shower, brushes his teeth then showers himself again in his favorite Ed Hardy cologne. When he walks over to his closet to pick out his gear, he couldn't decide which way to play it. A smooth white linen suit or a laid-back pair of jean shorts, an orange, blue and white striped Sean Jean shirt with white uptowns. He decides on the white linen suit, despite the fact they saw each other, they haven't really met, and he wants to leave an impression. Chance dresses quickly, as he realized how much time has passed and still must find the "package" he was delivering, which he was not sure what that was. After he dresses, he grabs his keys and he run outside to his car.

Chance had a 2002 black BMW with 22-inch Giovanna rims. It had a matching custom black and red interior. This car was his present to himself for his 18th birthday; although it was 6 years old you would never know it. Chance took excellent care of his car. He was at the car wash every week getting regular checks and tune-ups. He drove her nice and slow down the street, giving everyone a chance to break their neck from doing a double take.

Chance got a block from the hospital when he found out what his package was going to be. He pulls into the parking lot of cress florist, runs in, and grabs three of the biggest arrangements they had; asking the lady to put them together, paying for them and then leaving. Seeing the clock on his dashboard when he returns, Chance began to panic that he missed her since it was now ten minutes after three. Chance finds a parking spot right in front of the main doors, just as he puts the car in park, he sees Aubrielle emerge from the building and walking in his direction. "This is too good to be true, first the spot, then she comes at the precise right moment." Chance says to himself. Chance gets out of the car, and sees Aubrielle checking him out, he pops a peppermint star in his mouth to ensure freshness as he walks over to his passenger side of the car to get the flowers when he takes them out of his car everyone in the area is looking at him.

Aubrielle walks over to the bus bench and takes out a book, she acts like she is reading it, but she is really checking for Chance. She thinks back to the phone call earlier and how nothing came from it. She begins to think someone was just playing a mean joke on her. She silently begins to hope that someday someone would send her flowers like or even just a single rose, which no one has ever done before. All the sudden she becomes envious of that lady who is going to receive those flowers.

As she becomes jealous, she is awoken from her daydream from a strange yet deep and sexy voice saying her name in a tone that sang to her. She then realized it was the man with the flowers.

"Hello, Aubrielle, these are for you." Chance begins. "May I sit with you for a moment?" he continues.

"I'm sorry you must have the wrong person!" she says shyly.

"No, I have the right person. It is you that I am looking for." He replies.

"Really and why is that?"

"I wanted to ask you to dinner again." Chance looks at her as she glances over at him for the first time since he sat down, they make eye contact, Aubrielle flashes back to the day at the park and tries not smile.

Instead, she stands up as the bus approaches and says, "you have never asked me to dinner, I do not know you and I will not be needing these." she hands the flowers back to Chance and gets on the bus.

Chance is left standing on the corner holding the giant bouquet of flowers, not understanding why she is not into him and if he will ever see her again. So, without thinking twice he gets on the bus too.

The bus is pretty much empty except for the driver, him, Aubrielle and a few other people. He takes the seat next to her and tries again.

"You are right you don't know me; my friends call me Chance. Yes, I did ask you to dinner yesterday at the park. I know you don't need them, but I would like for you to have them, after all, I did buy them for you." Chance says, confused. He doesn't know how to play it; he never had to work at it this hard before.

"Why did you buy them for me, you don't know me. Aubrielle says coldly "Furthermore how the hell do you know my name and where I work?" she adds.

Chance reaches in his pocket and pulls out the business card her sister wrote on and holds it in the air for her to see her information in Annalise's handwriting. However, he doesn't hand it over. Just as quick as he pulled it out of his pocket, he put it back in. 'My sister gave him my information' Aubrielle thought to herself. I must remember to hug her for medaling, at least this time.

"Look," Chance begins. "I bought the flowers because I thought what you did for that little girl was amazing and I know we don't know each other but I would like to change that. Just one dinner. Let me take to one dinner, and if you don't like me or don't ever want to be bothered again, I'll leave you alone. You will never see me again, but please just give me a."

"Chance, that's cute use it often?" Aubrielle snaps

"Actually, no I have never used it before." Chance says blushing with an embarrassed laugh. He was impressed with how quick and witty she is. "Let's try this again, hi Aubrielle. My name is James. I was wondering if I may take you to dinner some time."

Aubrielle looks at Chance; he has a very gentle and sincere look about him. Before she can answer he leans in and kisses her on the lips. Aubrielle is torn not knowing what to do. She doesn't want him to stop but this is not the proper thing to do. She was not a virgin, but she was only with one guy in her life.

Chances pull away and abruptly say "oh my God, I'm so sorry." Aubrielle mind starts to race why is he saying this. He didn't want to. He didn't like it. In a low whisper, she says, "I must have done it wrong." Not realizing she said it out loud until Chances replies by saying "no, it was great. I just thought you would be mad me because you have to fight me off this whole time."

"Would you do it again?" Aubrielle asks bashfully.

11

Chance says "Yes, but only after you have dinner with me."

"How is tonight?" Aubrielle asks as she stands to get off the bus.

"Perfect. How about 9 pm – I will call you when I'm on my way." Chance says as he gently rubs his thumb over her cheek. Aubrielle agrees and hurries off the bus so he doesn't see the goose bumps her body is now covered in.

Chapter 2

After only stopping to get the mail out of her mailbox, Aubrielle runs to her apartment. She goes straight to the end table in her living to retrieve the phone off its base, to call Anelise.

"Anelise, speaking." Her sister answers her phone, always trying to sound important.

"How dare you give my number and place of work out to someone neither of us knows!"

"Brie, listen he seems nice, and really into you, and did you see him? He is gorgeous. You are not getting any younger; it's time to live a little. Go get a free dinner, maybe get laid no one is saying you must marry him. Wait, how did you know I gave it to him?" she asks curiously.

"Well, I could tell you know or when you come over to help me live a little," Aubrielle replies playfully.

"What? Come on brie what happen, you spoke to him? You are going out with him? You know I need details. "Anelise fires off.

"Well, hurry up and get here, I need help!! He is coming at 9 pm to get me." Aubrielle says urgently.

"9 pm, girl is you crazy it used to take a week for me to get ready. Meet me and Angelina at the salon 0n main street in 15 minutes." Anelise instructs her.

Aubrielle agrees and hangs up the phone. She runs to the bathroom to wash her face and brush her teeth, she then changes into her favorite orange velour suit, before she leaves to meet up with her sisters.

Aubrielle is one of three children born to Adrianna and Antonio Miakova, who were high school sweethearts and now have been married for 35 years together. They are still very happy and in love. Aubrielle would have given up on true love a long time ago if it wasn't for her parents. Every time her father walks into the room where her mother is, it is like he falls in love with her all over again. Her mother, on the other hand, acts like a little schoolgirl who just saw her crush for the first time when he walks in the room. Aubrielle remembers asking her mother once "what was the secret to their marriage. "Her mother replied, "Well, dear that is easy you must find someone who loves you a little more than you love them, so they always put you first."

Aubrielle sat back and thought about what she said, and it made perfect sense, but she couldn't figure out in her parent's marriage who was the one who loved who more. So, she probed some more.

"Well, who is it you or daddy?" she asks

Her mother giggles as she answers, "if it wasn't your father who was in love with me more, we wouldn't be married." She then stops and thinks for a moment before she continues "well, I guess that was in the beginning, but things change, and people grow sometimes together and sometimes apart. We were lucky we grew together. Although things change at times the love was always there."

"How do you keep the love?" she asked.

"Well, "I'm not sure; I think the fact that your father and I always accepted each other for which we are and never tried to change the other person helped. Instead, we work what we had and trained the other one to be the person we needed and taught each other to give each other what we needed."

This always stayed in Aubrielle' s head and she wonder if she has ever had this conversation with her sisters. They are all so different, so different in fact it is hard to believe that they are sisters.

Angelina is the oldest at 32 years old. She was a very successful lawyer in Nassau County, long island New York. She works at one of the top law firms, as a junior partner. She was beautiful; she stood at 5 feet 8 inches tall and was very thin. If she weighed 120 lbs. Aubrielle would be surprised. She had brown hair with natural reddish highlights that she has always worn in a bob style haircut. Her eyes were a warm inviting brown, like milk chocolate. Angelina never had a serious relationship more like a series of them. She was married to her career. She never dated a guy more than 6 months and always had 1 or 2 on reserve just in case she got tired of the main one quicker than she anticipated. In her case, they were always more in love with her than she was with them and the more she didn't want to be bothered with them they more in love they were with her.

Anelise, the youngest of the sisters, looked like she could be the child of Angelina and Aubrielle. She had Angelina hair color and height and Aubrielle curves and eyes, but her eyes weren't as shocking as Aubrielle. Annelise's eye was more of a blue-grey color. The feature that separated her from her sisters is the Anelise had long gorgeous curly hair. The kind of curls women would pay a fortune for at the salon for a perm. Only the perm always fried your hair and leaves you practically bald instead. Anelise didn't have a college degree like her sisters do; she barely made it throw high school. The night of her graduation she didn't even walk to get the diploma, as she went into labor with the first of her 4 children. Anelise is married to Javier the father of all 4 of her children, her high school sweetheart and the only man she has ever been with. Her children are 8 years Bentley, and then 6-year-old is Enzo. Javier named his sons after two of his favorite cars. Anelise names the next two Giana is 4 years old and their only daughter, and Avanti is their 8-month-old. Javier went along with it but Anelise found out later that is was only because they were the names of 2 rim companies Javier was fond of. Javier was a car salesman and was a genius at it. He could sell snow to an Eskimo. When they first hooked up it was Javier who was more in love with her, and today that is still true. Anelise is a great wife and a wonderful mother, she thinks of things her husband and kids need/want before they do, she has a deep connection to them.

Aubrielle got to the shop 20 minutes later, where faithfully both of her sisters awaited. They rushed outside and grab Aubrielle. "Come on, come on we have so much to do. Ok, Angelina, she is here you can go." Anelise directs.

"Wait, what? What is going on? Go where? Aubrielle asks

"Relax brie, get pampered with Lee. I'm going to go get you an outfit, or did you have something in mind already?" Ang asks.

"Oh, no I guess I didn't think of that," Aubrielle says concerned.

"Relax, I got this. I'll be back in ten minutes. Angelina says, taking Aubrielle credit card.

Angelina really meant she I will be back in ten she was no joke when it came to shopping.

Angelina and Anelise thought of everything. Mani-pedicures, facial, whole body wax, wash cut and blow out. They even arranged for her to have her makeup professionally done. Ten minutes later as promised Angelina came back from her shopping trip at the mall, with the perfect outfit. It was a soft brown wrap dress with the perfect pair of Louis Vuitton high heel sandals. These shoes not only made the outfit, but they were the defection of sexy. Angelina suggests she goes light with the accessories just the diamond hoop earring her parents bought her for her 16th birthday and the diamond tennis bracelet they brought her for graduating from college as an RN.

When they finished at the salon, they went back to Aubrielle's apartment where they still had work to do. Angelina ran to the store to get some refreshments in case she decided to have him come in after they went to dinner. Anelise stayed and cleaned up the apartment, to make sure it was in order if he came in. While Aubrielle jumped into the shower and finished getting ready, after the shower, she put on lotion and her favorite Burberry perfume. Then she touched up her hair and makeup and put on the outfit her sister just bought. The three sisters had a pact that anytime they had to get ready for an event that they wouldn't look in the mirror until the other two sisters looked at them first.

When Aubrielle walked into the living room her sister's jaws dropped. "Well?" Aubrielle pressed, but the sisters just sat there. "Well, how do I look? "She asked again, only to still receive silence. Aubrielle runs over to the full-length mirror in the living room to look at herself. "Well, dam she asks as she twists and twirls in the mirror looking at herself from every angle. The three of them begin to laugh, and Angelina says, "that is what we were thinking, you look amazing."

"You sure do, go get him, sis." Anelise adds, just as Aubrielle phone rings it's Chance's calling to let her know he was on his way.

Chapter 3

After Aubrielle left him on the bus, Chance got off at the next stop and took a cab back to his car. Where he immediately went to his spot where his boys waited for him.

Chance had many friends and acquaintances, but Dizzy and Blue were more than friends they were his family. Emmanuel "Blue" Shaw and Chance were friends from birth, their mothers were best friends since middle school. Samantha Shaw (A.K.A Momma Shaw) was Blues mother and Chance's Godmother. Chance went to live at momma Shaw's house after the death of his own mother. Since there was such a strong bond and lots of love between them Chance living there was the right thing and most comfortable thing for him at that time in his life. Chance needs to be with people who loved him, and it made him feel needed too. Momma Shaw had 2 other children besides Blue, the twins Mariah and Xavier, they were almost 2 when chance moved in. They were a handful so Momma Shaw needed as much help as she could get, and Chance was more than willing to help.

Blue was cute but nowhere as handsome as Chance was. He was short, stocky and always was his hair in cornrows that were in different designs, this week it was in a spider web because of the new spiderman movie being released. Blue started to work in a local store when they were in high school and managed to work his way up to a managerial position.

Dizzy, on the other hand, was the "Ugly" one of the groups. Maybe if he ran with a different crew it would be different but next to Chance and Blue, he had no chance. And he knew it; he would always say "hey there is always one ugly one in the group." Dizzy's real name is Cameron Jackson. His grandmother raised him. After, his parents divorced his mother had no use for him since she only got pregnant to trap his father. His mother didn't know that his father never wanted kids, and knew she was trying to trap him, so he ran away faster. Dizzy's grandmother nicknamed him dizzy because she said, "when he was a baby and cried to calm him down, she played Dizzy Guise music, and he would stop." She made him take up the trumpet in school, which worked in his favor he received a full scholarship to Five Towns College; right after he got the scholarship his grandmother was diagnosed with cancer. She said that this gave her a reason to fight, and to continue to live." Dizzy was the first in the family to go to college. His grandmother used to tell everyone "No one, not even the good Lord is keeping me from seeing my baby walk down that aisle to get his degree."

"What up man you're late, and you're never late?" Blue asked

"Yea man glad, you are finally here. So, what are we getting into tonight?" Dizzy asked.

Blue starts to inform Chance of everything that is going down tonight. What stars were making appearances at their favorite clubs, who having house parties, and any other get together he can think of.

As the three men sit in their barber chairs, (they each had their favorite barber; the barbers knew they had to be done together.) Chance replies "Sorry my dudes, I have other plans tonight." As his 2 best friend sits staring at him like a deer caught in headlights. Chance clears his throat and says, "I have a date." His friends, the 3 barbers and everyone in the shop waiting for their turn who knew Chance began to laugh. "ah, Chance I love you like a bother, you know my man but let me put this nicely you're not the type of guy that "Dates", and what the hell your banging' like 4 chicks now." Blue advises. Chance just looks at his friends and nods. Then he tells them about Aubrielle and how they meet and what happened earlier that day. Chance tries to explain that he wants to see what happens and to see if he can be an "honest man" even though he knows his friends doubt him. Truth is, He also doubting himself.

After they finish at the barber shop, they go to the mall to find him an outfit to wear. The walk around the mall and go into every store twice. Chance could tell his friends were getting mad because they always did everything together. When Chance was "Going out with" anyone else his boys were right there with her girls. So, the fact that he was going out without them was hurting them, and he knew it but wasn't going to let anything stand in the way of him and Aubrielle. Chance finally decided what he wanted to wear. It was a Kenneth Cole mocha suit with an orange shirt, and tie that had multiple shades of brown and orange in it, as well as brown belt and shoes. While he is at the register, he realizes that it was now 7:45 pm and has just enough time to shower and get on the road.

Thankfully they live 5 minutes from the mall, and Dizzy lives 2 houses down the road. Not that he is dropping him off at home anyway. All three men get out of the car, after taking out his packages from his trip to the mall he tosses his keys over to Blue and asks them to go to the car wash and to fill up the tank.

Chance comes out of his room 45 minutes later, Ready to go on his date. Momma Shaw is in the kitchen with the twins who are doing their homework at the table, and his boys are just walking in the door, Chance looks at the window and sees his car is safe and clean in the driveway when he turns to see everyone is staring at him.

"What are you all looking at?" he questions.

"Damn, you never clean up like that to take me out." Blue teases him.

"OK, ok leave him alone. Chance you look very handsome, she must be special." Says momma who finishes with "Kids get ready, bed is in 5 minutes." Momma instructs the twins.

"Thanks, Ma; I'll see you all later." Chance says as he runs out the door searching for his cell phone to call Aubrielle to let her know he is on his way.

Chapter 4

After Aubrielle hangs up with Chance, the three sisters start to make there was downstairs. "Wait, you never told me anything about him?" Angelina presses.

"That's because I don't know anything about him yet. I saw him yesterday at the park, he asked me to dinner I said no – Lee gave him my number without my knowing. Then today he should up at the job with the flowers and asked again." Aubrielle replied.

Anelise looks over at the two of them and says "Yea, but I don't get it, Brie. You acted like he was busted at the park yesterday. I'm mean did you even see him. That man is fine as hell, he burned my panties, and you just walked away. So, why today did you say yes?"

"I don't know why. I guess he didn't burn them until today." She says shyly.

"When he came to the job with the flowers. it was the flowers, weren't it?? Angelina pries.

They get out of the elevator on the first floor and start to make the way out of the building when Aubrielle replies.

"No, actually after he gave me the flowers, he got on the bus with me. Which was funny because his BMW was right there? When he started to talk normal, you know not with all that extra shit. I was about to say yes to his invitation to dinner when he kissed me." She explains.

"WHAT?!?" both sisters scream.

Aubrielle' s phone starts to ring, and its Chance. He is calling to ask her if he should come up to her apartment or wait there. She tells him she's walking out the front door now and will be right there.

When the three sisters walk out the front door, they see Chance leaning against his car. The moment he sees her walk out of the build he can't talk his eyes off her. As they approach him, he is still staring at Aubrielle but manages to say, "Good evening Ms. Anelise."

Anelise gets all giggly she can't believe he remembers her or her name for that matter. Chance stares at the card with Aubrielle information on it more than enough to remember the woman who helped get him here. "Hello, it's nice to you again. This is our sister Angelina. I hope you too have a great time." Anelise replies. "Hello Angelina, it's nice to meet you, I'm James." Chance says still staring at Aubrielle. Then he asks Aubrielle "Are you ready to go?" Aubrielle replies by nodding her head, then turns to give her sisters a quick hug with a simple I'll talk to you later before walking closer towards Chance, while Chance opens the car door for her. After opening the door, he reaches his hand out to help Aubrielle walk over to him. Just before she gets in the car Chance pulls her in his direction, so they are faced to face. "I can't take my eyes off you." He whispers to Aubrielle. She leans in and kisses him. As they stand under the streetlights, wind softly blowing kissing Aubrielle can her Anelise yell "Burn baby burn."

It was the first time that Anelise had kissed Javier. She was about 14 years old, at the time that a young lady body starts to change, and they notice. After she and Javier kissed and explored each other for a little while, she told her sisters she had to go to the bathroom because she felt like she peed in her pants but knew she hadn't." Aubrielle asked her if she was in pain, or if it burned because they were learning about STDs in health class in school. Anelise said no but they went to their mother for clarification.

"Ma, we are learning about STDs in school and we have some questions." Angelina began. Adrianna wanted to die this was hardly the conversation she wanted to have with her three little girls but was glad they came to her for their questions. Their mother told them about the birds and the bees, and basically, all the technical stuff that an adult tells a child because they are too embarrassed, to tell the truth. Her sisters began to ramble on and ask questions that Anelise really had no interested in because of the fear of having an STD.

"So, what does it mean when your panties get all wet, is it an STD?" Anelise asked her mother.

Her mother prayed for God to give her the correct wording to get through this, then began cursing their father out for not being here with her to get through this.

"No honey, it doesn't mean that. It means that she had a special connection to someone, and her body liked it. oh, my goodness what am I saying to you? You don't need to worry about this anytime soon." Her mother's response. 6 months later Anelise and Javier had sex for the first time. But it wasn't until years later that they understand the power of an organism. So, as they got older every time, they liked a guy or was attracted to a guy or even had great sex with someone they would say he burnt my panties as a joke.

As they drove away from her building, chance lowers the radio to make conversation, which he can't do over the heavy beats of the rap music he is playing. As he searches for some soft R&B on the radio, Chance asks Aubrielle "Is there anywhere special you would like to go?" she nods no, and he continues "I'm sorry I didn't think to make reservations anywhere." "That's ok wherever you would like to go is fine." She replies which she does mean but can't help to curse herself out for giving him such short notice. She is touched that he apologized for no reservations, and was impressed that he sounds like he wanted to take her somewhere you had to think ahead and call to get in.

"OK, I got an Idea." He informs her. He heads east on the Long Island Expressway; He heads to a small-town call Port Jefferson Station. It a little fisherman's town, it has cute little shops that line the streets, along with restaurants, and ice cream parlor. It's right on the marina, where the ferry that transports people back and fronts over the long island sound from long island to Connecticut.

Chance decides on a little restaurant, the atmosphere is romantic there are no lights in the restaurant other than the light from the Christmas lights that framed the walls and windows, and the candles on the top of the white linen tablecloths on top of every table. Chance orders a bottle of white wine. "Will that be okay for you?" Chance asks Aubrielle, she nods yes. "What would you like to eat?" Chance asks her. "Umm, I am thinking of the chicken marsala with extra mushrooms. What about you?" She replies to him. "Lobster, I love seafood. I don't get to eat it often." He says. When the waiter comes back Chance orders from them both. and again, she is impressed because he remembers to ask for extra mushrooms. Throughout dinner Chance and Aubrielle make small talk to get to know each other. Although he let her does most of the talking as he didn't want to give her a reason to run off which he thought she would if she knew all his baggage. Chance began to worry during dinner it seemed that every three minutes his phone would go off, he would just shift in his chair and hope she didn't hear it.

Aubrielle heard his phone alright, but she was happy that his complete attention was on her. Like they were the only two in the world, so she ignored his phone for tonight anyway besides way too early to be questioning him she thought to herself. As Chance pays the bill, he asks her "would you like to go for a walk down the marina and get ice cream, I know this great little shop they make it homemade, it's like velvet."

"Sounds great," she replies

Aubrielle is really enjoying herself and him, he is doing everything right. Opening doors, ordering for her and when they walked out of the restaurant it was chilly, so he took his jacket off and wrapped it around her. Chance saw her rubbing her arm to warm herself up, so he wanted to be gentlemen and take advantage of the opportunity to touch her. After wrapping his jacket around her, he pulled her close and they walked down the street with his arm around her and continued their small talk.

"Do you come here often on dates, or do you just love ice cream" she pries wanting to more of his dating history.

Chance hesitates. "No, when I was a kid my mom took me here before she passed away, now I take my God Brother and sister here when they get straight A's on their report card, which is rare. It is bittersweet for me to come here ~" I miss my mom so much it hurts to be here but makes me happy at the same time — so I reserve it for special occasions."

"I am so sorry James. I had no idea about your mom" she says hugging him

"There was no way for you to know, it was a while ago but still hurts and I rarely talk about it." He says shyly.

"I want you to know and feel like you can talk to me. no pressure just knows I am here and will listen." She says sincerely, and with warmth and compassion before Chance realizes it, he tells her everything.

Well almost, he tells her the basics but not the details of the murder or his drug-dealing ways. He starts to wonder if she thinks it anyway the way his phone is on fire tonight. Now chilly after ice cream and the breeze coming off the sound. Aubrielle suggests they leave. She hugs him, thanks him for letting her in to understand him even a little bit, and they embrace. They linger there to look out across the sound, the night is so clear, the millions of stars in the sky light up the water and you can see clear across to Connecticut. As she turns to walk away, he pulls her back for one more kiss under the starry night sky, this time more urgent, and more passionate. She loves every second of it.

The whole ride back to Aubrielle' s apartment Chance's hand was on Aubrielle somehow; whether holding her hand or rubbing her leg. Aubrielle for sure was falling in love with his touch, it was sweet, urgent, passionate, strong, and his skin felt so soft like cashmere. When they get back to the apartment, Chance asks to use the bathroom. She takes the opportunity to light candles. She loves candles, the way the smell, and the romantic way the light flickers. She figures this will add to the mood. She takes his blazer off for the first time since he wrapped her in it. She inhales his cologne and then hangs it up, takes her sandals off, and makes her way to the kitchen to make a pot of coffee. She begins to fill the pot with water when she feels Chances hands around her waist, his breathe on her skin, and his lips on her neck. Her knees shake, as he whispers, "should I stop?" Aubrielle fights to get words out, something comes out, but it wasn't quite English or even gibberish. She pulls away blushing with embarrassment, only for him to pull her back in; kissing her on the lips this time and slowly makes his way to her ear. His hands move across her body, lost in his trance. Tet again he whispers, "should I continue?" as he pulls her in harder and tighter. Again, she can't get the words out, so as quickly as he grabbed her, he let go and began looking around her apartment. Standing there confused and pissed she asks, "why did you stop?" He replies, "I asked if you wanted to continue you didn't say yes." going to grab him she shouts, "and I didn't say no" but then realizes she still has the coffee pot in her hand, she turns to put it back on the counter, leaving her back exposed to him. He seizes the moment and sneaks back upon her, this time with the same urgencies and passion as on the marina. He doesn't stop to ask her anything this time. He walks up on her presses his hole hard body against her. She quivers as the goose bumps begin to rise. Chance begins to kiss the back of her neck, moving all around her neck, shoulders, and ears as his hands caress her body. He makes his way to the tie on the side of her dress and undoes the ribbon, making the garment fall to the floor. Aubrielle thanks her sister silently for stopping at Victoria's Secret[a] and picking up a matching lace bra and pantie set; not only did they match each other but her dress as well. Chances grabs a handful of her hair, having full control over the movement of her neck now. As he continues to kiss on her throat, he pushes his hard dick into her as much as he can, pulling her hair and making her turn around so they are faced to face. He kisses her lips and sucks on her bottom driving her mad. Just then, chance stops again, says "we shouldn't do this." Aubrielle is beyond pissed says "Are you serious? Why?"

"I don't know," he confesses. He wanted her more than air at that moment, but he was letting his feeling spook him, as his boy's voices echoed 'you not that type of man,' but he wanted to be that type of man; the man she deserved, but he knows deep down he would break her heart so he pulled away.

Chance stared at her floor hoping she would jump him right there, but instead she picked her dress up and said, "you know where the door is." Covering herself with the dress, she turns and walks out of the room. Chance gets a glimpse of her eye, and sees her confusion, and hurt, and knows he fucked up. It is starting already. 'I hurt her by trying to spare her from that. everything,' he thinks to himself. Knowing he should leave her alone because he was going to break her heart, but he could bear that look in her eyes, or leaving her broken-hearted, and remembering how insincere a woman mind is. She is not thinking that he caught feelings, she is thinking she did something wrong, or that he thinks her body is ugly since he stopped the minute the dress fell to the floor.

Chance unbuttons his top button and loosens his tie before he goes to her. She is in her room hanging her dress up on a hanger, still just in her panties set. Chance is memorized by her beauty, turns off his boy's voices in his head, quietly takes his shoes off and in one quick quiet motion takes his shirt and tie off. He puts his hand on her stomach, reaches around to her side and violently pulls her to him. She looks down refusing to make eye contact, but Chance is not trying to hear it. He lifts her chin with his hand, and they make eye contact. She is clearly hurt, confused, and mad at him. He tries to kiss her. She tries to pull away, but he holds her tightly. Desperate to make this right, he tells her the only thing that he could think of, the truth. "Aubrielle, yesterday in the park I fell in love with you. If I wasn't sure then, I am damn sure of it now. I feel things for you, and when I am with you, I never felt before. I am scared to love you, to lose you, or worse to hurt you. I never want to see you look at me the way you are now. I love you – I am in love with you and it scares the shit of me."

That was the first time a man said that he was in love with her. She felt it, she believed it, and she had to have him. She reaches up on her tippy toes to put her arms around his neck and hugs him, he kisses her arm, as he reaches up and grabs two fists full of her hair to pull her head back so her whole neck is exposed. He takes his time kissing every inch of it. Her toes begin to hurt from the arch he has her entire body in, as she tries to step back, Chance in one swift move only using his forearms picks her up, sending her legs in opposite directions as far as they would open, and lays her on the bed. There are at the top of the bed, but chance begins to kiss lips and presses his bulge against her to make her crazy with anticipation and to show her how much he wants her.

Chance works his way down, stopping to take her bra off, and then her panties. He keeps the same rhythm of kiss, lick, bite, and nibble all the way to her core. Aubrielle lost her mind before he even got there. He stops and pays attention to all the right spots on the way that had her scream with joy. Every time she thought 'I had to have him know,' he would find another spot to build the mounting excitement and desire. By the time he is between her legs, she was ready to run away. To keep her locked right where Chance wanted her, he put his arms under her knees and grabs her arm right above the elbow paralyzing her movement. The moment his lips touched her vulva she screamed with passion; her pleasure oozing down her legs, or at least the little bit chances mouth missed.

It was clear he was on a mission, and it was her. Before long Aubrielle eyes were rolling, toes were curling, and she was screaming at the top of her lungs. Her barley heard Chance when he asked, "whose pussy is this?" When she didn't answer his tongue became more aggressive working her body who such sweet power, that she began to convulse, yelling for him to stop only to have her request rejected. "Nope, not until you answer me, whose pussy is this?" Chances says playfully.

Body shaking uncontrollably, trying to free her arms between eye-rolling and toe-curling, Aubrielle manages to scream "yours" as she reaches her climax. As he finishes drinking her love for him, he releases her arms and climbs on top of her; quickly removing what little clothing he still had on[b]. The moment he slips inside of her, a tear falls down her cheek. Chance kisses her tear away, asks "don't you want me to stop?"

She shakes her head no. "Are you ok, am I hurting you? He fishes for answers, as he slowly moves his body back and forth.

All she can do is shake her head, no.

"No what – you're not ok – or I am not hurting you?" Chance asks more urgent.

"You're not hurting me" she whispers barely.

"Why are you crying then" he questions.

"I love you," she says, pulling him in to kiss him. Chance was overtaken by her omission. He gave her the best performance of both of their lives, and when it was over and they both reached their climax this time Chance didn't want to move, so he didn't, he stayed right there inside of his woman and they slept until morning.

Chapter 5

When she woke up in the morning, from the sun that was peeking in the window, she looked around and found chance was not only up but was watching her sleep. "You look so beautiful." He said as he bent over and kissed her forehead. She giggles with delight that he is still here. well that he is there at all. "Have you been up long?" she queries.

Chance shakes his head no, as he continues to kiss her. "I have to get ready for work," she states. She looks over to the clock to see how much longer she has before she should get up; just as she looks at the clock it begins to buzz its 5 in the morning.

"I got to go get ready for work!" she repeats the obvious.

Chances says "uh-huh, five minutes then we can get up, ok?" still kissing her. Before she can answer they are having sex again, this time he turns her over on her stomach, she is lying flat as he enters her, with each stroke she sticks her ass more in the air, this drives chance so insane that in a few quick powerful strokes he busts the nut that has been building since their last encounter, Chance didn't pull out nor was she on the pill but it didn't accrue to her to mind, her only thought was being late for work.

Aubrielle gets up, and goes to the bathroom, she showers and does everything that entails getting ready for the day including put makeup on which she never does. As she emerges from the bathroom chance is in the kitchen, she hears him snap "it's over, stop calling me." She sits on the bed, to put her sneakers on and process what she just heard. Questioning herself as to whether say something before she can decide chance, already dressed comes in the room with a cup of coffee for her.

"When do you want to leave- ten minutes?" he asks

"No, five the bus comes in fifteen minutes." She replies

"Are you crazy? "Chance snaps

"What," she says

"Do you really think I'm going to let my woman take to the bus to work?"

She didn't think he would take her to work or even pass last night, or really processed any of this yet. The confused look on her face must have said everything thing she was thinking, and Chance read every word of it.

"You really think I would let my girl, take the bus, and be around other dudes so they can try to talk to you – hell no – I'm taking my girl to work! He states.

"Your girl?" she asks, hoping she heard right.

"Yes, mine girl – you had no problem screaming it last night." He jokes.

She starts to explain "ha – we didn't talk about it, so I just thought that-" When chance interrupts her, "you thought what – that it was a one-night thing? That I told you all of that – things I never told anyone for some pussy?" he says pissed.

"No, I just honestly didn't think of any of this yet and we didn't talk about – what next?" she explains

"What do you want to be next? Oh, I see. do you have a piece of paper and a pen?" he asks

After looking at him stupidly, and him acting like he is writing on his hand to explain what a piece of paper and pen are, she goes and gets it. He turns around and writes on the paper and hands it to her. Aubrielle laughs and says "yes."

"So, you and me – you're my lady!" He confirms

She shakes her head yes again "but that works both ways – just me and you – exclusive, no side bitches" she replies

"Agree. now hurry I have to take my woman to work and she can't be late!" He orders – she laughs and grabs her stuff. As her head for the door, he grabs her "I don't want anyone but you; I'm going to change your life." Chance confesses.

It's been six weeks since their first date. They are together all the time, Chance drops Aubrielle off to work, picks her up and even spends most of her lunch breaks with her. They are together all day on her days off, and Chance practically moved in, as far as Aubrielle was concerned they were living together, but chance has made the official move because of his parole – that she still doesn't know about. Chance keeps telling her "baby, I don't want your parents to hate me. and they would if would move in after such a short time, but I wish we could make it official." However, he does have the key to her place and a bunch of his stuff is there.

Aubrielle is happy, and it shows. She is walking different, talking different and it is seen by all. All her friends and coworkers are jealous of her new man. They knew something was up when she started to wear makeup, then when she disappeared during her lunch breaks, and then they started to see her getting dropped off and picked up – not to mention the flowers Chance randomly sends her at work. She thinks he does it because he is thinking of her, but he really does it, so dudes know she is taken.

Aubrielle was a private person; she was far from the open book type. She is really one close to her 2 sisters and her friend,

Shavon. However, even Shavon doesn't get the whole story of Aubrielle' s life anymore.

Aubrielle and Shavon have been friends for years; they went to grade school and nursing school together. They even work together at the hospital. Although no one understands why they are friends, they get why Shavon is friends with Aubrielle but not the other way around. Aubrielle is a sweet woman, who is very loyal — so loyal it is a flaw. Shavon, on the other hand, is very selfish, she doesn't do anything that doesn't benefit her in some way. For example: If you were lying in the street bloody, she would turn around, and walk away so not to get blood on her shoes. Shavon is only loyal to herself, not even her man, Marcus; they have been together for eight years and for all eight years she has cheated on him with one man or another, and it doesn't stop with men. Attention is better than no attention at all was her life's motto.

Today, when Aubrielle got to work she was extra sparkly. Chance bought her a diamond and ruby heart pendant with a white gold chain it hung from. The heart was huge, bigger than a silver dollar piece. Chance gave it to her last night, he said: "I gave you my heart and I want the world to know it." He also told her he had it made just for her.

When Aubrielle walked into work wearing that necklace, to say that Shavon was pissed is an understatement, envy was not something she wore well.

"So, if this dude is that all that, why have you introduced us, I am your best friend?" she demanded to know.

"I don't know. We are not at the stage of meeting each other people, I guess. I am still getting to know him myself." Truth is told she knows better than to bring him around Shavon after all the only other man that Aubrielle had sex with was Marcus.

It was their senior in high school; Marcus was the star basketball player. They were approaching the finals and he was failing chemistry. He had to get a "B" on the midterm or would be bunched for the rest of the season. He asked Aubrielle to tutor him, and he got an "A". He played in the game, and they won. To his surprise and everyone else's there were recruiters for the NBA in the audience, who came there to see him. Shortly after the winning game, he was signed to the Knicks, after his meeting to sign with the Knicks, he asked Aubrielle to dinner. They began to see each other, they had sex a handful of times but there was something missing. She never told anyone they were seeing each other, other than her sisters. Aubrielle always acted like she didn't care which way it went, although she did like him. Aubrielle did not want Shavon to know that they were dating, but she found out.

It was Aubrielle's birthday, Shavon was on punishment but since they were BFF's and their parents knew each other well. Shavon's mother allowed her to go to the party, mainly because she knows the kind of girl Aubrielle was, she knew there would only be family there. The truth was she wanted Aubrielle to rub off on her daughter because she saw nothing positive in her daughter's future. During the party, Shavon took Aubrielle's phone to call her mother, to check in and wanted to use her phone so it would come up on the caller I.D. and her mom would know they were together. After she hung up with her mother a text message came through from Marcus. "Hey sexy, can't wait to see u, miss u"

And true to form of Shavon the ugly green monster came out; there was no way in hell she was going to let the star of the high school, a future NBA player with a contract for millions date anyone but her.

On the low, she began to pursue Marcus, and after a couple of weeks of her endless attempt and numerous lies about

Aubrielle being out with someone else or anything to get him to think she was cheating, they became a couple. Aubrielle wasn't mad though, because as far as she knew Shavon knew nothing about her relationship with Marcus.

Even now she is not mad, even with the 6- diamond engagement ring, {which is the 4th one, she sold one after a fight, lost one, and left one at her lover's house that of course he said was not there), the mansion with 8 bedrooms, the maid, the driver, he gave her the world. She only worked to pull the wool over Marcus' eyes. To make him think she was a good woman when she wasn't. She only worked to entrain herself is what she told him since she refused to travel with him and the team because that was her free time to do what she wants. Plus, now she can spend his money and save hers. Please, it gave her a social setting to find her next victim or an excuse to not be home when Marcus was checking for her. It seemed more that Shavon wanted to be her friend because she envied her life and the peace that came with it. Aubrielle always thought she was insecure, but Shavon was far worse when it came to that too. After, having a front row seat to all her drama, Aubrielle kept her distance and learned a lot from Shavon's mistakes.

Today at 3 o'clock, when they got off work, instead of running to her brand-new range rover, that Marcus just brought her. In her sneaky bitch fashion, she popped up on Aubrielle and Chance, when they were in the parking lot. She stayed her distance and watch Aubrielle her "best friend "walking to the parking lot. Chance always the gentlemen got out of the car to greet her and open the door for her. This pissed Shavon off, even more, then when she realized it was a BMW with customer interior her blood pressure raised, when she saw him, how beautiful he was, and his body plus the green eyes – she went over the edge and was bent on making him her next victim.

"Hey Brie, wait up a sec" Shavon calls out, as she walks over to them. Aubrielle was pissed; she knew she was just being nosey. She smiled when she turns in Shavon direction – not because she was happy to see her, but because Chance wrapped his arm around her and kissed her forehead, then when she looked up at him he kissed her lips right in front of Shavon. Then she took her pocketbook and other stuff she was carrying, out of her hand and walk away to put them in the car – Aubrielle was now beaming since clearly, he had no interest in her. Now Shavon was infuriated, walks pass Aubrielle and say, "since clearly, you're not going to introduce us, I'll take matters in my own hands."

"Hello, I'm Shavon – Aubrielle' s best friend or used to be until you came along," Shavon says.

"Well since you're her best friend, then you can understand why I want to spend all my time with her." Chance says, then introduces himself "you can call me Chance."

"Ok you meet him; we have to go we are going to be late. "Aubrielle informs her.

"Dinner plans" Shavon pries

"Yes, I have a date with GG and a boxing lesson with Bentley tonight, so it was nice meeting you, but I can't let my peeps down." He says

"Oh, dinner with the FAM?" Shavon questions her, with a mean glare, remember her comment of "were not at the meeting each other's people phase yet"

"Yes—I'll call you later, "Aubrielle says as she walks and gets in the car.

Chance follows in suit and they are off, while Shavon was still there even more pissed that her friend dismissed her, and her new victim is not interested. As they drive away Chance takes Aubrielle' s hand

"Babe, please tell me that is not really your best friend," he asks

"Why?" she asked back

"Because, she is a fake ass bitch, all up on my dick and smiling in your face like that." Are his responses.

"She is always like that, don't stress it or let it get to your head." She demanded "Wait, do you want to fuck, or would you?" She asks paranoid

"I wouldn't fuck that HO with that crackhead dick." He says pointing to the obvious crackhead walking down the street. "She looks like she is a gold digger, selfish ho who fucks everyone." He finishes as he pulls into Annelise's driveway.

Chapter 6

When they pull into the driveway, Annelise's 3 oldest children are playing in the front yard. Aubrielle hated when her sister let the kids play in the yard, the street they lived on was a very busy, and dangerous street. Besides you never know who is watching your kids, especially when you are not. Even after Chance turned the car off, Aubrielle sat there admiring her niece, and nephews playing. Chance leans over, kisses her forehead and says, "no worries love, that will be us one day soon." She smiles at the thought and even more because chance is thinking of their future too.

They get out and the kids come running over, they love their auntie and get excited to see her, as she does with them. As Chance, Aubrielle and the kids make their way to the front door Anelise popped her head out the kitchen, to say hi and tell everyone to wash up dinner was almost done.

"Will you please help me wash my hands Chance?" GG begs, she loves Chance, and is always asking for his help, she won't let anyone else help her when he is around. "Of course," he replies, as Bentley screams out "last one to the bathroom is a monkey." "Come on g- baby we'll see you inside, GG and I don't want to be a monkey- right," he says looking a GG- "no way – I hate nanas" GG replies, making an ugly face. They take off and of course beat everyone else to the bathroom.

40

As Aubrielle walks into the house, she says hello to everyone. Angelina is also there with her latest boy toy, Demetrius. Demetrius is the new district attorney, she really seems smitten with him, and he is head over heels in love with her like the rest of them. He is very handsome and has he stuff together which of course is a stamp of approval in everyone's eyes.

The Knicks game is on as Aubrielle' s father Antonio, Javier, Javier's best friend Wally, Demetrius and Chance, who joined them after he finished helping GG, Bentley, and Enzo are all hovered over the TV. Her mother and sisters are in the kitchen putting the finishing touches on dinner. Aubrielle goes over to her dad to catch up with him, her parents must meet Chance before, and they really seem to like him and how happy her daughter has been, nonetheless her father wants to check in. As she is talking to her father, she overhears the conversation between Javier, Wally, and Chance.

"Yea that is Brie's best friend's man," Wally says he also went to school with Javier, Aubrielle and her sisters.

"We were all so pissed when that ho, Shavon stole him from Brie." Javier chimes in.

"What the fuck do you mean stole him?" she demands from Javier "sorry, daddy for my mouth." She says like a little bashful girl, she hates cursing in front of him, and he disapproves of it more. "What do you mean stole- she didn't know we were together – I didn't even know you knew that." She says piercing Anelise with one of her death looks; she cannot believe her sister told him.

"Brie, I'm sorry, everyone knew. Marcus would brag all the time that you were his girl, he was into you – it was not a secret – and she dam sure knew." Javier said both apologetically and obviously at the same time.

Aubrielle was beyond pissed off, Chance was studying here to figure out whether she was pissed about losing the millionaire NBA player or the betrayal of her best friend of 20 years.

"I was told that at your birthday party she used your phone to call her mom to check in and a message popped up from him and she read it," Wally explains

"By whom," she asks as her head is spinning

"I used to fuck with her cousin. Remember? Josie??" Wally says direct but playful.

Just with his comment the party, and how Shavon's attitude change when she came back in from calling her mom came back to Aubrielle's memory, and how she never got that text from Marcus – she found out later when he called her back to ask why she never answered – that bitch must have erased it. These little things from that night came flooding back to her, making complete sense to what she was just told. Her mother, who was still in the kitchen with Angelina, just came through the swinging door that separated the kitchen from the living room letting in the aroma from tonight's dinner, Fish. The smell goes right through Aubrielle, who now is dizzy and has the sharpest pain in her stomach as she feels the hot vomit rising in her throat. Aubrielle runs to the bathroom to let it out.

"Wow, she is really upset over homeboy, huh?" Wally jokes

"No", her father says "loyalty means everything to her, and she just found her best friend shat on her – that Shavon is a piece of work, a real piece of shit. You're lucky you haven't met her or must deal with her! Poor Marcus." Her father says to Chance, shaking his head.

"Sir," Chance always is extra, to her father. "I met her today, and your right, she is a piece of work. Brie and I were talking about how fake she was when we pulled up, she is worse than a dude." Chance states "I'm going to check on her." He excuses himself.

Chance opens the bathroom door and can't even see her head it is so far in the toilet. She is violently throwing up. "Baby, are you ok? This bitch got you bugging, I'm so sorry." He tries to comfort her, as he walks over to her. Her mother and sisters come in a right after.

"No, no it was the fish." she answered, "the smell made me sick." She explains then goes back to throwing up.

"What you mean?" Chance says confused

Chance looking confused "it's ok James – go inside with the guys watch the game, she needs her mother right now, ok?" Her mother continues as she pushes him out of the bathroom.

"But I don't want to leave her." Chance tells her

"It's ok, she knows you're here, just give me ten minutes with her, ok? Then I'll come to get you when she is better. Go ahead go now." She says and closes the bathroom door in his face.

Her mother goes back to her, but Chances knocks on the bathroom door. Angelina opens the door "I just wanted to see if she was ok yet?" Chance asks in a boyish manner.

"Baby I'm fine – I need a minute, I'll be right out please going watch the game," Aubrielle says, holding back the new puke rising in her throat.

"Ok, but I'll be right outside; if you need me please come get me, Ms. Adrianna, Anelise, Ang someone? Please come get me." He begs.

"Of course, we will," Angelina says, then closes the door.

"My, he is quite smitten with you," her mother says, as she wipes her far head with a cold washcloth. "So, the fish, huh?" she asks her daughter. All Aubrielle can manage to do is shrug her shoulders.

"Well how long has this been going on, have you thrown up before?" her mother quizzes as she sits up, and shakes her head no.

"I haven't thrown up in years." She says

"Well, when was your last cycle?" her mother continues the quiz

"Ma, why you are asking all these questions?" Aubrielle questions her mother back.

"There is no doubt about it she is pregnant!" Anelise screams

"Shut up, no I am not" Aubrielle fights back.

"Well, prove it. Take a test. I have one in my draw, and I'll be right back," Anelise says dancing

"Ma make her stop" Aubrielle pleads.

"Well dear, a little piece of mind never hurt anybody, right?" her mother says, as she rubs her back.

"I can't be. I just can't be" Aubrielle says more to convince herself more than anyone else in the room.

Anelise walks out the bathroom, and Chance is still there "is she ok Lee, what is going on?" he asks.

"She is fine, she wants to brush her teeth – I'm going to get her a toothbrush, can you do me a favor, please? Can you guys feed the kids, and start eating we will be right in – 5 minutes ok?"

Chance just nods yes, as she gives the same instructions to Javier and the rest of her guests. The guys go to the table, Anelise goes to get the test and returns to the bathroom, she hands Aubrielle the test.

Before Aubrielle even finishes peeing on the stick that shit turns bright blue. Aubrielle' s heart is pounding through her chest when her mother takes the test from her, the hold it up for her sister to see.

Before she even has a second to process it the lawyer in Angelina comes out. "What are you going to do? What is Chance going to say?" were the only two questions she could rattle of before Aubrielle holds up her hand to stop her, she begins to cry.

"Ma, don't be mad at me." She pleads

"I am not mad at you, honey. I do wish that you guys used protection and waited a little while longer but nonetheless the baby is on its way so we can't change the past, only move forward and prepare for this blessing. Your father and I love you very much and will be here for you and our grandchild." Her mother replies, with a smile.

Our grandchild, a blessing that was the stamp of approval Aubrielle was seeking from her mother. Her sisters knew that too, as they began to sing "we are going to be an auntie.", as Aubrielle, and Angelina did the four times before for Analise's babies.

"Shhh, I don't want Chance to hear." Aubrielle snaps at them.

They look at her confused. "You're not telling him?" Anelise questions

"No, not yet – I want to go to the doctor and make sure everything is ok before I tell him, and I want it to be special." She informs them.

She makes them promise not to say anything, which they do. She tells them that they have plans for dinner tomorrow; she will confirm with a doctor tomorrow beforehand and then tell him after dinner. Then Anelise gives Aubrielle some Vicks vapor rub on a trip to stick up her nose to block the smell of fish to make it through dinner after she applies it, they go to join the rest of the family. Chance is still pacing around when they emerge from the bathroom, running over to her he fires off with the questions "you ok? you want to stay, or go?" before

45

she can answer her mother interrupts "baby go have a seat, mommy will make you some soup – it will be better than fish with that bug you have."

That made her feel better, Chance will think she has the stomach flu for now, she doesn't have to eat the fish and when Anelise went to go get the test she light candles and open windows to get the smell out, so it is now so overwhelming, and the Vicks is getting rid of what is left of the smell. Everyone has been so worried about Aubrielle now one noticed the way Demetri had been starring chance down, not even Chance. However, now that Aubrielle is ok, and things are calm, everyone is trying to get to know Demetri. After a few questions directed at Demetri the next blow of the night comes.

"So, Chance what is it that you do? Demetri enquiries.

Just then Aubrielle realized she didn't even really know the answer to that, she knew he had money but didn't know how he got it. Funny thing is her sisters never asked either, with the car, clothes they way he wined and dined and spoiled Brie they all knew he had money. Aubrielle starts to panic within she doesn't even know the father of her child.

"I am not working right now – I guess you can say I'm in between gigs right now, I got laid off – company downsizing," he says so matter of fact like the sky is blue.

"Well, what about rent and money?" Demetri presses, which is starting to piss Chance off. He hates people that are nosey as fuck.

"Well, if you like you can pay my bills!" Chance snaps to put him in his place, but everyone thinks he is joking so they laugh.

Aubrielle looks at her mother with panic in her eyes, she is pregnant, and her baby daddy has no income kind of panic. She knew she had money and they would be ok for a minute; she is far from a gold digger. She has no problem holding them down, but it will not stretch far, and when she has her maternity leave, they will lose her pay when she is out. This is all too much for her to take in.

Her mother steps in the conversation to clarify things. "So, James is you ok seriously?

Chance knows that he must come down to talk to her mother, so he exhales and begins his story – of course, enough details that they feel sorry for him but not everything, so they still have respect for him.

"My mother was murdered, when I was 18 years old, on my birthday actually. She was walking from the parking lot into our apartment, she was walking slowly because she was carrying a lot of things, including my cake. Birthdays were a big deal to her" Chance begins to say while looking down the whole time. "she was hit in the head with a stray bullet, she was laying in the parking lot in between two cars, I found her a little while later, she was barely hanging on, as we drove in the ambulance we had our last talk ever, which is ironic since it was the best talk we ever had too – she said" I knew you would come, I waited for you – I had to tell my baby boy happy birthday I am proud of you. I love you with all my heart – I told her I loved her too and begged her not to leave me – you're all I have is all I kept saying don't leave me, the last thing she said is I will always be with you. Right after that she flatlined, the EMT began CPR by that time we were in the hospital parking lot between the EMT's and hospital staff they did CPR for 30 minutes but it was pointless, she had no blood left in her body, but I could not stop crying and begging them to save her. They said she could have lived if someone found her body 20 minutes sooner if not more, but it was July 6th, my birthday and people were still partying from the 4, so no one heard the gunshot over the fireworks that were going off. I now hate both days and never celebrate – I don't even leave

47

the house these days. I just can't, I can't do it. my mother had a life insurance policy and some other assists that she left to me – stocks, bonds, etc., so I have money. Her best friend who is also my godmother took me in after that, so I don't pay rent or bills like that – I do give her money to help her out though. Since and my mom had been best friends since they were in diapers and her oldest son and I have been best friends all our lives, it was a bittersweet move. I know they love me, they are the only family I have ever had other than my mom – she was adopted, had no siblings, and I never knew my pops or her adopted parents they died right after she graduated from high school. – so now there my family, that is my momma and my brother and the twins- my little brother Xavier and little sister Mariah – I owe them a lot because who knows where I would have ended up, and without them, I would have no family."

Everyone was quiet for what liked forever, all the ladies wiping the tears from their eyes, and her father just shaking his head yes – like he really admired Chance now. No one knew what to do until GG saves the day "yes, you do have family James – you have me and auntie Brie and all of us – right auntie?" she says will her angelic face, and sweet smile as she clings to chances neck. "Right baby –we are his family now too."

"So, can we have a really big party for your birthday chances – I promise to make your birthday special again– please auntie brie – please Uncle James. She begs with that smile, and when she called him Uncle James his heart melted, and he replied, "well as long as my family is there."

"Well duh," GG said giggling, and he kisses her forehead and then Aubrielle. To stay in tune with the conversation Javier jumps in "hey bro – come down to the lot tomorrow – I can hook you up we are looking for new people – I can put in a good word and shit." "Language!" Anelise corrects him.

"Word, you would do that?" Chance says.

"Of course, we are family," Javier says – they all laugh and look at GG who is shaking her head yes. Demetri and chance give each other a look, which quietly states this, is not over yet.

Chapter 7

The next morning, still feeling sick Aubrielle calls into work. She tells Chance she is going to the doctors to check it out but assure him it is nothing. "Ok cool, make your appointment and then I'll call Javier to see what is up and if I can go at that time, so I can drop you off and pick you up when I'm done at the lot. Then we can go to mama's house for dinner – they are dying to meet you, and I told her not to cook fish." He tells her with a laugh. "Oh ok, I thought we were going out to dinner." She says. "Well they have been asking and asking I didn't think it would be a problem." He responds

"No of course not, I can't wait to meet them." She tells him

Aubrielle made her appointment for 3:15 pm and he made an appointment with Javier and his boss, the owner of the lot Dexter for 3:30. They get dressed and leave the house according to their plan; she just got dropped off and is filling out the paperwork. She is freaking out, hands shaking, sweaty palms- she is a mess.

Chance gets to the lot and is just as much of a mess as Aubrielle, but for a different reason. Dexter didn't even interview him. "Javier put the good word in for you, vouched for you- so that is good enough for me. Next week you can start, Monday through Friday 9-5pm for orientation, then the schedule comes out weekly there are three shifts 8a-4p or

50

12p-6p or 2p-10p. The routes and hours will vary, you must wear slacks, bottom down oxford shirts with a tie always and dress shoes – you must dress for success. Any questions?" was all he said – "No right now" Chance says.

He is just so happy to have a real job, to be legit, and to get his parole officer his back that he doesn't care about anything else. He says thanks to Javier and that he will talk to him later and racing to find Aubrielle at the doctors to tell her the great news.

Chance is in the waiting room since Aubrielle was already in the exam room when he arrived. In the exam room, they take her vital signs and ask a million questions. "So, what brings you in today?" Dr. Mandina asks her

"I think I am pregnant. She states

"Why do you think that? When was your last cycle?" Dr. Mandina quizzes

"I think May 8th, "Aubrielle says and then tells her about the fish smell and throwing up, and the test.

"Have you had dizzy spells, tired, any other symptoms?" Dr. Mandina continues.

"Yes, I guess I just didn't put it together until now," Aubrielle confesses.

The doctor requests a urine sample, Aubrielle complies with the request. Then the doctor does an exam, they made small talk, they know each other from the hospital. Aubrielle always like Dr. Mandina she had a great bedside manner and was professional yet caring.

Then the doctor confirms her pregnancy "yup, your pregnant, make an appointment for next week and we'll do a sonogram if your dates are correct you almost 7 weeks, you can make the appointment with the front desk, and I'll see you after the soon, congrats. "the doctor says

"Thank you," Aubrielle says beaming; she takes a second to process the info then texts her sister.

"Hey chick, I need a huge favor" Aubrielle texts Anelise.

"Hey, what up what did the doctor say and what is the favor? Anelise replies

"First, I am pregnant – almost 7 weeks, I'll have a sonogram next week to confirm, 2 can you tell Ang and mom? I must go with Chance to mama Shaw's house for dinner so I can't talk now – but tell them I'll call as soon as I can. 3- can you get balloons streamers in pink and blue and whatever else you can think of and decorate my apartment, so when we get done with dinner and come home, he will see it? There is $200 in the coffee can, you know where to find it take what you need." Aubrielle pleads

"Yup I'm on it – congrats Brie – I'm SOOO happy for you and I get to be an auntie." Anelise texts in response.

She deletes the messages – checks her appearance in the mirror and goes out to the waiting room, when chance sees her, he is immediately on her feet. "you ok?" he asks, "yup just a bug – no worries, I just have to make an appointment for my annual physical for work – can you get the car and I'll be right out?" she asks. He shakes his head yes, kisses her cheek and exits the building. She makes the appointment and is out right behind him.

She climbs in the car "so, what happened at the lot." She asks

"Big things baby, I got the job – Javier really hook me up." He states, "for the first time in years things are looking up, and I see a future, I know my mom is smiling down at me." He says with a hint of sadness in his voice. She takes his hand and holds it all the way to momma Shaw's house.

Momma Shaw's house is adorable, not at all what Aubrielle thought it would like. It is small ranch, quant yellow, with white trim and blue shutters with a match front door and flowers everywhere. Momma Shaw really loves her house; it's obvious by how well it is kept.

Aubrielle is in deep thought first about them having a house like that to raise their baby in, and then to his family and whether they will like her. She is so deep in the thought she didn't even realize that the car was off, and Chance was holding the door open for.

"ummmmm, hello, you going to get out. He asks, "what are you thinking of?"

"I'm sorry, that I love her house and what if she hates me. She blurts out before she realizes it

"Impossible, she is going to love you. And I promise we will have a house just like it." He says smiling at her, he wraps his arm around her and guides her into the house.

As they walk into the house Mama Shaw is in the kitchen cooking, the twins are at the table doing their homework and his boys, Blue and Dizzy, are outside lighting the BBQ. When the door closes behind them, the twins get up and run over to Chance. He begins to play around with them; it is clear the love they have for each other. Aubrielle is delighted as she admires the way he is with the kids, the same way she does when he is with her niece and nephews. "No, horseplay in the house" mama yells from the kitchen. In unison Chance and the twins scream back "sorry, ma"

"Baby, this is my little man Xavier, and my lil shorty Mariah or x and rye as we call them- guys this is my lady Aubrielle." He introduces them

Just then his boys and mama walk into the living room – "hey guys this is my lady Aubrielle, Brie this my mama, Blue and Dizzy." He says.

"Hello, it is so nice to finally meet you; Chance is always talking about you." Momma says, as she gives Aubrielle a hug.

"You're so pretty." Xavier tells her. "Awe, thank you X." she says. He giggles in approval, he loves that she called him "X", instead of his full name like most adults would do.

"Do you have a nickname too?" Mariah curiously asks

Aubrielle answers "yes, my sisters call me Brie, and if you guys like you can too." She winks at them, Mariah nods, this makes her feel special.

"Well, Mrs. Shaw please let me help you set the table." Aubrielle offers

"No, not unless you call me momma." Momma Shaw says through her laugh

"OF course, momma." Aubrielle says with a warm smile, now feeling special herself. Just like that the Shaw house is back to normal, with the new addition to their family. The kids remove their books and homework from the kitchen table and go to the coffee table in the living room to finish their work, as momma shut the TV off then leads Aubrielle to the kitchen. Chance and his boys go back outside, they play around for a few minutes like there are 12, and then talk about Aubrielle, Chance is seeking their approval.

"Well, see is something else." Dizzy says looking at Blue and Chance in disbelief

"What the hell does that mean – by the look on your face it can be a good thing." Chance says

Blue answers for Dizzy "nah man it is a great thing – she got you, the kids and momma of all people to fall for her in the first 10 seconds upon meeting her, and it is easy to see why."

Dizzy continues "yea, she is sweet and dam she is fine. So why are you still fucken around with these bum bitches??"

Chance looks away and just shrugs his shoulders. "You need to leave her alone man; she is too good of a girl for you – it isn't right." Dizzy finishes with

Chance gives him a look to shut the fuck up or get fucked up.

"Chill, both of you, we are boys, and we have your back Chance, he just means that you can't lead a double life, it WILL catch up with you. again." Blue informs him.

"Yes, man and that chick is a keeper – so keep her or move on." Dizzy finishes Chance just shrugs his shoulders, he knows what they are saying is true but he still doesn't want it to be - after they said what they needed to say they all go back to playing around like little boys. While Aubrielle finishes the table and momma Shaw finishes the dinner, she is in the middle of taking out the food of the over, when she tells the kids to put their stuff away and get cleaned up when the doorbell rings. She can't imagine who that can be, so she asks Aubrielle to answer it.

"Sweet can you get that, it's probably UPS." Momma Shaw says. Aubrielle nods yes and goes to the door.

Aubrielle opens the door and is surprised when it is not UPS. Instead she finds a heavy-set middle-aged white man. His is very bald on top with 5 pieces of hair to brush to one side; thick coke glasses with black plastic frame outline his eyes. He has on a short sleeve white button shirt- that is buttoned wrong, and only have tucked in, with khaki pants that are three sizes too big, that he holds up with a red belt. To finish off his look black easy spirit sneakers and a pocket protector filled with pens and a name tag hanging around his neck that is backwards. "This man is a hot mess." She thinks to herself.

"Hello, may I help you?" Aubrielle begins

"Yes miss, my name is Edgar Moore; I am with the New York state parole board. I am here to see Mr. James Curtis; I am his new P.O and I need to meet with him. Edgar states, as he is telling her this chance comes in a look for her, momma told him she went to answer the door, as he walked to the door he heard enough of Edgar response to Aubrielle, to know she knows the truth.

Paralyzed with this information she just stands there. "Is he here?" Edgar continues. Chances walks about behind her and puts his hand on her back, she moves away from him, but stand there it is clear he is a liar and wants to hear what this man should stay. Chances heart sinks: she has the look in her eyes of hatred, confusion and being broken.

"Yea I am James." He tells Edgar

"Great, I'm Edgar Moore your new P.O, sorry to bother you at dinner time – but after all these years you know the drill, I just need a few moments of your time may I come in." Edgar asks

"No, I'll come out – brie waits here." Chance says

"No, please come in Mr. Moore." Aubrielle says

Chance is pissed, he knows she is looking for answers and this is not how he wanted her to know.

"Thank you miss. Again, this will be quick. I was assigned to your case this morning, so I wanted to introduce myself. It says here on your file that you have been home for about 2 months after serving just short of 4 years in Hudson correctional facility, upstate – is that correct?" he asks

"yea." Chance whispers looking only at Aubrielle. She swallows hard, and fights back the tears forming in her eyes, as she looks at her feet. Her baby is all that she can think of, and how could he not tell her something like this.

"I'm sorry to hear about your mother, I see they never did find the person who shot her, or answer any of the rumors that surrounded it." Edgar continues

"That is true." Chances states.

"Rumors?" Aubrielle says confused

"Yes, that Mr. Curtis was really the target, but since he was not home – they shot his mother to make him suffer instead – revenge, you know." Edgar says extremely cold.

Chance is pissed off "you need to leave now. You know nothing about my mother or me for that matter – I don't give a fuck what that file of you says."

She has never seen him so irate. It scares her; she walks out of the living room. Momma is coming in her direct, when she hears Chance scream at this man. "Aubrielle what is going on – who is here?" then she looks at Aubrielle face "honey is you ok?" momma asks. Aubrielle shakes her head no, and the tears come pouring out of her eyes – she screams for Dizzy and Blue and directs them to go check on Chance, and to the twins to eat, as she takes Aubrielle in her room.

"What happened?" she asked, "who was that?"

Aubrielle is trying to come up from the tears she is drowning in to answer when blue comes in and tells his mother, "Chance's new PO." She shakes her head, understanding now why Aubrielle is upset. Momma and Chance had this conversation two days ago; momma told him he had to tell her before she found out another way.

"He lied to me." Aubrielle cries out, rubbing her stomach. Why would he do this to me?" she asks.

Momma looks at her "oh hunny, he loves you, he was trying to protect you and himself. He is afraid to lose you and afraid of the past."

Shaking her head, no, Aubrielle can't wrap her mind around it, of any of it. "Is it true, was his mother murder because they wanted revenge on him."

"they never found the guy who shot her, we don't know why it happened – we don't know anything, but we do know that shooting happen there daily." Momma tries to explain, this world was new to Aubrielle, she says the effects of it in the

ER, and on the news. However, she never knew anyone who took or Sold drugs let alone the things they were talking about now – she felt like she was in a bad movie.

"So, it is just as possible, as it is not possible." Her quires

"I don't know how to answer that Aubrielle, I guess so if you just want to look at the negative." Momma snaps back.

"It is not the negative momma; it is the realistic point. I need to know what I am involved in; it could be me, or our baby." Aubrielle answers, rubbing her belly.

"You're pregnant?" she asks

"Yes, I found out right before we came today. He doesn't know yet, he thinks I have the stomach flu– I want to tell him in a special way, but I don't know now." Aubrielle says dazed.

"Having second thoughts?" momma Shaw asks trying to see where her head is.

"I want to go home now." Aubrielle says "I'm sorry; I just want to go home." She says crying

"Ok, I'll get Chance, you need to talk to him Brie, and you need to tell him." Momma Shaw suggests.

"No, can I call a cab?" Aubrielle asks.

Just then Chance barges into the room, "no, what do you need a cab for?"

"Chance, she would like to go home, this has been a long day full of a lot of information plus she is sick." Momma Shaw defends.

"Baby please I just want to talk to you." Chance starts to plead with her; he goes to lift her head, so she will look at him and not the floor. But she jerks away, "I want to go home alone." Aubrielle demands. "Ok, I will take you" he starts to say, she shakes her head no. "Yes, I will take you, and get you home safe, I'll drop you off." Chance states. He walks out of the room to get her pocketbook and his keys.

Momma walks over to her and hugs her tight "if you need anything- anything at all you call me – promise me and before you decide anything." Momma pleads with Aubrielle, she just shakes her head yes, and thanks her as she goes to the car to wait.

Once outside she leans against Chances car since the door is locked, some random girl walks passed her, a few times before Aubrielle turns to her.

"Can I help you?" Aubrielle asks – hating this question since it just ruined her left the last time, she asked it and can't deal with whatever this girl should say.

That is when she noticed her necklace; the girl asks" where Chance is at?"

"Who are you" Aubrielle asks

"What is it to you?" the girl snarls at her, and then sees her necklace – it is the same heart.

"I'm his girl, that is who. Why are you looking for him?" Aubrielle asks the girl.

"yea aren't we all" she chuckles, then turns and walks away, not before Chance see the exchange, and runs out there to do more damage control. As she sees him, she walks away quick and goes back into the house across the street.

"what did Heather say to you?' chance snaps at Aubrielle, "who, oh you mean your girl – the one you had a necklace specially made for – guess you had them give the mold so you can make the same piece of shit for me." She snaps back, ripping the necklace off her neck and throwing it in his face.

Just then Wally came driving down the street, when he sees Brie he stops "what up guys?"

Aubrielle is so relieved to see him, she doesn't even answer him, she just gets in the car and locks the door – "take me home" she barks to Wally.

"drive!" she demands again. Wally does what he is told, as he looks at Chance as he pulls off.

"You ok, Brie?" he asks as they get down the street

"no." she shakes her head.

"Did he put his hands on you?" he asks

Puzzled by this question he took at him stupid and responses "hello no, we got into a fight I'm pissed but dam isn't that serious – and don't tell Javier again it is not serious – couples fight."

"Ok, as long as you are alright." Wally says

She shakes her head yes and looks in the mirror to see how bad she looks. Thank god not that bad – her makeup is in place, although her eyes are puff. "You feel better from last night?" Wally asks.

"Kind of now, I throw up this am too – I went to doctors and it's just a bug." She says, as he pulls in front of her building. She thanks him, again tells him they just had a disagreement and it's not serious so no need to worry everyone. Then exits the car and goes up stairs as quick as she can, when she walked in the elevator to go up to her floor, she could see out the front door of the building and sees Chance pull in. She wants him to come in and just as badly wants him to stay away. She goes into her apartment and sees the decorations that Anelise and the kids put up. She did a beautiful job there is balloons, streams, and banners everywhere. On the wall, right when you walk in is a huge sign that says congrats Brie and Chance with the kid's hands and feet prints all over it. Aubrielle began to cry, her cell phone rings it is Chance, she cries harder, and ignores it. She feels so defeated, she just wants to shower and get in bed. The whole time she is in the shower Chance is blowing her phone up – she finally texts him back, in a very direct and clear manner "leave me the fuck alone!!" she sends – even more pissed that she was put in this position and then thinks of the

60

baby. It is bad enough her sisters and mother now know and she shamed with a baby out of wedlock with a man she has known for barely 2 months, she can't shame them more with an abortion, there is no way she can carry this baby for nines to turn it over to someone else. "What do you think sweet pea." she says rubbing her stomach, as she sits on the side of the tube, in just a towel when the doorbell rings. "She ignores it, she knows it is not Chance he has the key, and she don't want to be bother with anyone else, she is longing for him and hating him all in one – to say she is torn and confessed in the ultimate understatement. Just then she hears the door open and close, she emerges from the bathroom. Chance is standing in the living room; he is looking all around in aww, with tears in his eye. "I came to get my stuff, since you want me to leave you alone! You sent that text message knowing you were carrying my baby. You weren't going to tell me?" Chance says now crying. Fuck that she thinks – he doesn't deserve compassion and how dare he flip this shit on me, also pissed at her for not ripping this shit down like she wanted to but couldn't find the energy. "I'm going to be a daddy, that is why you were sick" Chance says, like he had a "uh-huh" moment. "no, you're not going to be shit, no get your fucking lying cheating ass out of my apartment!" she screams with fire in voice, tears in her eyes, and vomit in her throat. She runs out of the run to the bathroom to release it from her throat. Chance is right behind her, but she slams the door in his face. She lies on the bathroom when she finally finishes, the tile is cool against her hot skin, and her head is spinning round and round like the cyclone of a tornado. When she comes out of the bathroom, hours have passed, and it is pitch black both outside and in the apartment. Chance left, she has no idea when and she is even more mad – he knew I was sick, and he just left. She thinks looking for her pajama's bottoms and one of his wife beaters to put on. After she dresses, she goes to the kitchen to get a drink, when she opens the fridge, she sees it stocked with ginger ale, and there are several boxes of saltines on top of the fridge. She smiles, her sister thought of everything.

She sits at the kitchen table – where there are cards on the table, she opens them – she sees her mother's handwriting and begins to cry.

> *Hi Baby*
>
> *You don't have to call tonight. Take the times to cherish this moment with James.*
>
> *I will call you tomorrow – love you*
>
> *Xoxo, Mommy*

The second card is a printout of the baby furniture she has been in love with, since Anelise was pregnant with Giana.

> *It will be delivered in two months – daddy and I wanted you to have a Chance to clean out the guest room and paint first.*
>
> *Love you, mom –*

the note on the side of the picture reads. She is pissed that she just opened their baby's first present and he is not there. She goes to the window and sees his car is not in the parking lot. Scared, mad and confused she cries all the way to her bed. She cries herself back to sleep for hours. She is woken up at 2am with stomach pains; she looks around the apartment and then goes to the window and still no chance. She goes to the bathroom, and continuously throws up until 4:30 am. "geez, I don't understand how I have anything left in there to come up, you got to calm down in there – we can't spend the next few months like this." She says to her belly. Then thinks about how she has got to get up in two hours to go to work, she starts to dry have, "fuck this" she thinks and for the first time ever she calls in sick to work.

Chapter 8

Chance has been outside of Aubrielle's apartment since 4:45 am, he left the apartment after she locked herself in the bathroom, and couldn't get in there for 2 hours so he went to talk to momma, the only person who can calm him down right now, and help make sense of this. After speaking to momma, he didn't feel any better – all she could say was give her some time, give her the time to sort through all of this. She is hurt. Chance was annoyed at first. He thought it was at momma, but he couldn't be. She was just telling him the truth – he fucked up, he hurt her he can't blame anyone but himself. After tossing and turning in his bed for a while he got up and went back over there – I'll just wait for her to come down to go to work. She is carrying my baby, no fucken way she is taking that nasty bus to work. He thought to himself. When 6:50 am rolled around and Aubrielle still had not come downstairs, Chance went up to her. He found her on the bed with a box of tissues, and dirty tissues on the floor, with the phone in her hand and throw up all over the bathroom, then cleaned the entire apartment, he had nervous energy so he was working off. After he finished cleaning the bathroom he jumped in the shower and climbed into bed with her. He was so worried about her, Aubrielle was so anal when it came to a clean apartment or her environment, so for her not to care about what a hot mess it was, and missing work. Chance finally started to get just how bad she was hurt.

He holds her as tight as he can, as they lay there and slept. When he woke up, he would just watch her – not just because of how beautiful she was to him, but he was checking to see if she was still breathing. It was after 2 in the afternoon before she woke up. That was not like Brie at all – she barely slept, she woke up every day at 5 am if she was off or not, and didn't go to bed until 11pm every night, and went all day longer, no naps – shit she barely sat down he thought. When her eyes open, she looks around confused she finds Chance and their eyes lock, he brushes his fingers across her cheek.

"You ok? You got really sick again last night." Chance says concerned

"No, why are you here?" she replies.

"I came back this morning to take you to work, but you never came down, I got scared and came up to check on you?" he whispers, surprised that she let him get all of that out.

"And you decided to stay because?" she burst out as he finishes

"the house was a mess, in the bathroom there was throw up from one end to the other – I got worried and was not leaving you, so I cleaned the entire apartment and took a shower and came to lay with you and our baby." He said rubbing her belly. She was too tired to push his hand away, and to fight. Her exhaustion physically paralyzed her.

"You ok now?" he ponders – she shrugs her shoulders. "Well I went and got you ginger ale and saltines last night they say that will help. I also ordered you Chinese food; wonton soup is good when you're sick. Well at least that is my mom did when I was sick. I'll get you some." Chance says gratefully, since she hasn't told him to get out yet. As to goes to get up, she whispers his name "James" he turns back to her, as she tries to pull him back he goes to her, pulling her into his arms – she rests her head on his chest and sobs uncontrollably for what seems like hours. All he could do was hold her and say "I'm so sorry Brie; I love you" repeatedly.

After she finally stops crying, Chance tells her everything – he leaves nothing out, missy, the murder of his mother, his drug dealing, why they thought he had something to do with the murder and even that he still deals."

"What the hell do you mean, we are always together?" she says

"I don't touch the drugs – it is through a 3rd party." He claims

"I don't understand." She tells him

"I don't touch the drugs – I invest my money into them – my dude sells them with my money and then gives me back the money with interest. For example: say I give them $5000 of my money, he will make $13,500 roughly and if done right, he gives me back 10 doubling my money and keeps the $3,500. So, if anything ever happens – as far as I know I just let a friend borrow some money" He explains

At least his hands are clean now, he is not out there on some corner, and addicts will go anywhere to find it. Aubrielle tries to justify this to herself. So, the drug thing is not that bad – but his mother's murder – if that was revenge and I am his girl carrying his baby, what is to say that we will be ok. And what about chick that lives right across the street. Chance can see her mind is still racing, and still confused, and pissed.

"What happened to no side bitches?" Aubrielle presses.

"what are you talking about- I haven't been with anyone but you, you are my girl, you are all I want." Chance tries his hardest to convince her.

"yea, right – that's not what your side bitch said, when she was wearing my necklace that you had "made for me" wasn't that what you said?" brie argued

"yes, it was and is special, but I didn't have it made. That chick, Heather, she has lived across the street from us for years. I never messed with her, she is jealous that is all, her having the necklace that is just a coincidence "he tells her

"I don't believe you!" she says pulling away from him.

"Brie think about it. What did she say? damn sure didn't say I'm fucken him or that she was my girl." He barks at her, getting pissed.

"She did – she asked for you, I asked her who she was she said who am you- I told her I am your girl and she said aren't we all." She barks right back.

"I do not want her – I never did – I was never with her, never tried to do the things I am trying to do with you with anybody." He says as he pulls her back to him, she doesn't fight him, she just lays there. They lay there in silence for a few minutes when Chance brings up the baby. "what do you want to do about the baby?" Chances ask her.

"what the fuck do you mean?" she says, as she begins to cry.

"last night when I found out that you were pregnant – you said I wasn't going to be shit – I thought you were having ideas to end it or give the baby away." Chance tries to explain

"that is what you want so you can back to your bum bitches?" Aubrielle snaps at him.

"Dam Brie – how many times do I have to tell you I want you!! What do I have to do to prove to you that I want us, this baby, and I want you to be my wife and the three of us a family? and if we add to it, it will be with more kids." Chances says, "Marry me, Brie." He says, looking straight into her eyes.

"No, chance. I love you but I can't, and you are asking me for the wrong reasons." She says.

"My reason is I love you and want to be with you." He says defensively

"I am pregnant, you're a drug dealer on parole, who may have been the reason his mother was murdered, and you have been cheating on me – all of this in one day this comes to light." She said, "your reaching."

"I did not have my mother murdered." Chance says with fiery in his voice. "Fuck, I didn't mean it like that, I was just recapping everything. I'm sorry" she says reaching for him "I don't trust you; I don't feel safe and I don't want you to marry me because I am carrying your baby." She continues "this has been going so fast, all of it, and I am not complaining but I don't know you but now I know you are not the man I thought you were. I need time."

"I am the man you that I was, I am the one for you – I am James with you, I don't have to be anyone else Brie. Chance is who I am or who I was on the streets in order to survive, you're the only woman that has ever been real, your love is pure and unconditional I don't have to pretend with you – if anyone knows me it is you, you are not leaving me because I am not letting you go." Says Chance

"Don't ever fucken lie to me again, or hurt me b or our baby, I will not allow to hurt our baby, because if you do – I swear on everything that you will never see us again." She informs him.

"I promise you; I love you." Chance tells her.

For the rest of the evening they stay in bed, holding each other, making love, watch old movies. Chance quietly thinks to himself ways to make it up to her, while she doubts everything, and can't shake a bad feeling she has, and the intensity is terrifying her. "I am going to change your life." Is all that is echoing in her mind, the first promise that Chance made to her.

Chapter 9

It has been a week already, since her last appointment, and the day of truths as Aubrielle calls it.

Today is the day of her sonogram, she is so excited. They extended offers to her parents, momma Shaw, her sisters and his boys to go to the appointment.

The appointment is not to the afternoon, they had to wait for everyone to get off from work. Aubrielle and Chance leave early to go to the store to get him clothes for work. Yesterday, was his first day and he enjoyed it, he said he loved hanging out with Javier all day. This was bittersweet to Aubrielle, she knew he would keep an eye on him, but they were supposed to be at work not hanging out. He picked out 10 dress shirts, 10 slacks, 30 ties and a few pairs of shoes, with 4 belts his bills came out $1,8624.32, Aubrielle' s jaw dropped. She was so exhausted lately that when they go to the store she sat down and passed out. Which was fine with Chance, he knew he was a pain in the ass to shop with he was very particular to say the least, plus he knew how tired she was. He woke her up when he went to check out, everything was at the counter expect a box of shoes, and a teddy bear for the baby he was carrying. She thought he couldn't find anything good. "do you really need $2 grand worth of clothes?" she questions.

"yes, you must dress for success, plus I will have clothes for 2 weeks if we don't get to laundry often, with the baby and all. Relax baby, money comes and goes, and I still have plenty to take care of you." He tells her, continuing "as a matter of fact, maternity wing next, you're going to need clothes soon too." He reminds her.

She is just not into shopping, she isn't even that far along, but already has gained over 10 pounds, she is tired and doesn't want to try anything on and hates these clothes they are like tents she kept whining. She finds her way to the chair again and lets Chance shop for her. Another 2 grands in clothes for her, but he runs everything out to the car, so she doesn't know what they spent. He comes back in the store to get her; she is up and moving around now. See told you nothing good." She tells him. "I did you get you stuff, I put it in the car already. Do you want to go to the baby department and then to lunch before your appointment – we have two hours?" he asks. She says ok. She begins to look at everything and gets overwhelmed, nothing is for both sexes anymore. Everything is pink or blue no other colors of the rainbow. Chances goes crazy in the store he buys everything in both boys and girls. "Chance what are you doing?" she says when he racks up another 5 grands. "relax, what we don't need we can take back." Chance say, "I know you like to be prepared – so this is a start."

A start what the hell, then Aubrielle starts to cry thinking of her sister's house, although it is clean there is kids' stuff from one end to another, and that is with 4 rooms in the house being the kids. Bentley and Enzo share a room, Gianna, and Avanti have their own and they have a playroom plus not to mention the whole backyard and garage. "why are you crying?" Chance says worried

71

"you have seen my sister's house this baby is going to take over my little apartment." She cries. Chances laughs at her and hugs her grabbing the bags they walk out to the car.

They were in the baby department for over an hour, Aubrielle suggest drive through food, she hates to be late, Chance agrees. They stop and get food, and then head across town to her appointment.

Traffic is insane today, and Aubrielle is getting inpatient, she must pee and thinks they are going to be late. Chance dips off the main road and takes the back roads, and there it is the house that Chance has loved since he was little, the real estate agent just pulled out an open house sign when he stops, "wait her for a sec." he tells her." we don't have time for this, I'm going to pee all over your car, and my doctor is expecting us." She whines "two seconds" he replies.

As he gets out of the car the real estate agent stops walking up the driveway.

"Hello, my name is Dolly. Are you looking to buy" she asks?

"hello, I am James, is it for sale? He asks

"yes, it is, just came on the market, this was our first open house." She replies. Just as the owner pull in the driveway, they left the house during the open house. The agent introduces them.

"Are you interested" Mike the homeowner asks

"yes, I have been in love with this house for as long as I can remember, I was going to buy it for my mom before she passed away, and now my lady and I are expecting our first baby. How much are you asking?" chance asks, just as Aubrielle walks up.

"$250,000" mike response "what don't you come look around?"

"great may I please use your bathroom? Aubrielle begs

"oh of course come on, congrats on the baby, don't you just hate how the pee sneak up on you- one minute your fine and then next it is like you have been holding it for years." Carol, mike's wife says laughing, Aubrielle agrees, and laughs with her as she follows her to the bathroom.

Her and Chance look around, it is a beautiful house brand new kitchen, and bathrooms, hardwood floors throughout the house, it has five bedrooms, 3 ½ bathrooms, finished basement, 3 car garages, with an apartment above. Plenty of room to grown, please all the details, the mooring and fixtures it is beautiful. She looks at Chance, her eyes are huge with excitement.

"Can I make an offer?" Chance says, "is there any wiggle room?" he asks

"well depends on what you are talking about." Mike replies

"I'll give you 175 in cash right now – do you take checks? Chance tries to low ball the owner looks at each other, they want to sell badly, and move up north where their family is, their oldest daughter is expecting, and carol mother has fallen ill.

"if you can do 185 in a bank check – then I'll take it." Mike response, as carol nods in approval

"Great, we have a sonogram appoint in twenty minutes, I can go to the bank right after that, can we meet back here in an hour and half – say 3 o'clock." Chance suggests

"we can do that." Mike says as him and Chance shake hands.

As they get into the car, Aubrielle pauses and looks hard and long at her future and in this moment, it couldn't be any better. They decide not to say anything yet, this week was the fourth of July, and Chances birthday – GG has been planning his party with Anelise and the annual 4th of July BBQ – they figure they will tell everyone then, but right now it's about the baby.

At the appointment, they find out she is 8 weeks now, due on valentine's day, it is twins! As Dr. Mandina is showing the two separate babies chance say" so what is that: point to something on the screen. Dr. Mandina say "do you want to know the sex?"

Aubrielle laughs, "kind of late for that doctor, wow look at my son." She looks over at her father, who is beaming she knows he did want a son, as much as he loved his girl every man wants a son.

"so, we are having two sons?" Chance asks

"No, it looks like a boy and a girl" Dr. Mandina corrects him.

Now, Chance is beaming with joy, everyone is crying with joy and Aubrielle is laying there in love.

Chapter 10

After the annual 4th of July BBQ and chance's birthday party, things began moving quickly again. Aubrielle thought they were moving in on August 1, thankfully Mike and Carol are moving out on July 15, so they will have the place a little beforehand to get in there. Everyone helps, with picking colors, fabrics, lines, dishes, even landscaping which was left up to momma Shaw.

Chance has been killing it at the lot, in the past month since he has been there, he has sold over 20 cars. Today he has a surprise for Aubrielle, after he picks her up from work, they go to the new house they haven't been going over there in about 2 weeks. It is overwhelming for brie – she wants to do everything to prepare but can move a piece of paper from one counter to the next, without falling asleep. Chance had the house professional cleaned and decorated with everyone's ideas she approved. Today when she was at work, he had the moving company go to the apartment and move everything to the new house. They don't ever have to go back to the apartment again, Ms. Adrianna went there and cleaned it, handed the keys in and the moving company took everything. Chance, Antonio, Anelise, momma Shaw, Dizzy, Blue, the twins and Angelina put the whole house together in the eight hours Brie was at work. Every box was unpacked – the house was beautiful, right out of a magazine. Even Javier and Wally came through to help, Javier even bought the new black escalade with 22-inch Giovanni rims that Chance bought for brie, that was parked in the garage with a bright big red bow on it for her. Her family is sitting on the porch when they pull up to share in this moment and have a family dinner planned.

Aubrielle is amazed and feels so loved and blessed at his moment in her new gorgeous house – that she approved of, everything was perfectly done for her OCD ass. She was thrilled she didn't have to do any of it, packing, moving, cleaning even the decorating and even happier her family was here tonight.

"So, Brie I just want to say that if want to use Wally as a name- it's cools with me? Wally tell hers, making everyone laugh.

"Have you thought of names yet" Anelise asks

"No, not really." Chances says she he rubs her belly

"Will actually I have, baby." Aubrielle interjects.

"Oh, well do tell "he says

"Well, our daughter is Joanna Adrianna Shaw Curtis – she looks at Chance, her mother, and momma Shaw who are standing next to each other. "after her grandmothers" she says. The two-woman giggle with delight, and Chance hugs her stomach.

"And our son should have a name of strength, that is why he will carry the name Antonio James Shaw Curtis. Her father was balling just as hard as the woman. "they are perfect." Chances says and everyone nods in agreement.

"hey- your mother had the intimal thing too." Angelina points out, Chance nods his head.

"Yea, you said you wanted to keep that going too baby, I just thought our daughter would be "A" and son with a "J" and then the Shaw Curtis was a beautiful surprise." Chance says.

"This still is and gives our babies names meaning and represents our family. Brings your mom to it and gives my father the son he always wanted. I also thought that Angelina and Blue can be our son Godparents and Anelise and Javier can be our Goddaughter parents. Dizzy, I promise you got number #3" she says. Again, everyone cries and nods in agreement.

That night when everyone leaves, Chance runs the bath for her, "hey babe, I'll clean up I ran the tub for you to go soak and get off your feet." He tells her "but first I have a surprise for you." She giggles, "baby you did enough already." She tells him as the leads her to the garage. He tells her to walk in it, as she does, he turns the light on. When she sees the truck her jaw drops. "baby – this is beautiful but way too much. We have been spending like crazy – you have to take this back." She whines, as she checks it out.

"No, this is just as particular and as need as the house. Our hours are different, and although they have worked thanks to Javier bringing me to your job to drop off the BMW when I should work the 2-10pm it is not fair to you to have to get up and leave the house at that hour to get me, and not fair that he has go in the opposite direction to bring me home which is time away from his family. Plus, when the babies are here, not only will they look too cute in their matching car seat I already installed he opens the door to show her but what if you have a doctor's appointment or something. We need two cars, and safe cars for you and my babies." He testifies

"ok you made your point and I love it. Thank you, baby," she tells him.

They hug – he tells her to go take her bath now, and he will finish the cleaning up. When he finishes, he goes to find her? Aubrielle, is in the tub, candles lite, soft music playing from the music tv channels, chance had to have a tv in every room. He goes over to her, and gets in the tub too, Aubrielle is trying to wash her hair, chances take over and finishes it for her. It is so heavy and thick that she just can deal with it. She loves the way it feels when he messages her scalp and asked him to do her back. – Aubrielle feels so good right now, she takes his hand and moves it down forcing his finger side, she is trying to kiss all over him, and wants to make love to him, his finger is just not working, she moves his hand away and turns around and sits on his lap. "wait babe let's get out." He suggests. She shakes her head no, they make love in the tub, when they finish, she can barely move, these twins are sucking the life out of her. So, Chance, picks her up, helps her dry off and puts her in bed.

The next morning, after she dress and gets ready for work, she goes and wakes chance up. "she is pissed" baby it's 6:30 I got to be at work soon – get up." She whines

"Brie, I bought you a truck yesterday remember? He says sleepy.

"oh right. I'm sorry, well wake up anyone – I got a few minutes before I have to leave." She says kissing on him, Chances laugh and complies with her request as he think this pregnancies thing is so weird either she is too tired to move or horny as hell. –but nonetheless he was not complaining. After making love, they talk about the day ahead.

"you are working 2-10pm tonight- so what about dinner?" she asks before she leaves.

"eat before I get home – I don't want you and the babies waiting until ten o'clock for me- there is left over from last night. Let's finish that today – we are both off tomorrow we can go shopping tomorrow." He suggests. She shakes her head yes, and then just sits there. "what's wrong, did that wear you out?" he says with pride.

"No, Shavon comes back to work today from her leave. I haven't seen her since the day in the parking lot when you meet her." She says, she went on a trip with Marcus, they let her come and go as she pleases because he donates so much money to the hospital." she explains.

"don't stress that bitch, she hasn't even call you since she has been gone – some best friend she is." He reminds her.

Aubrielle goes on the explain why she is anxious "I know baby, this will be the first time I see her though, since I found everything out about Marcus, and everything that is new with us, the house and babies."

"Just try to keep your distance, I don't want her around you or the babies." He informs her, but goes on to ask her "are you mad about losing Marcus?"

Aubrielle stands to fix her clothing, as she shakes her no, but can't help but wonder thee same thing now that he mentioned it.

Chapter 11

Aubrielle pulls into the parking lot, everyone is breaking their heads to see who this is pulling in, and tint is too dark to see in the truck. Shavon is one of them; she pulled in about ten minutes before and was on her cell with one of her boy toys. Aubrielle is still stressing running into her, she wants nothing to do with her, and wants her to know why but doesn't want to deal with her.

Aubrielle parks and gets out of the vehicle. When Shavon sees it is her she hangs up on the toy and jumps out of her own car and goes running over to her.

"So, I see a lot has changed in few weeks." She says snippy. Aubrielle laughs, grabs her stuff and begins to walk away to get in to work. "Wait hold on. What is up with you – I'm your best friends remember." Shavon pleads, grabbing Aubrielle arm.

"You are not now, nor were you ever a friend of mine. Get off me." Aubrielle snaps at her.

"What the fuck does that mean." Shavon says, as she tries to pull her back, but Aubrielle pulling in the opposite direction and drops her bag, some of the contents spill out. Including the very popular read for a first-time mother "what to expect when expecting" falls out.

"You're pregnant?" she questions Aubrielle, with pure anger and envy in her voice.

"Yes, a lot has changed in a few weeks. I got a new truck, I am pregnant with twins due on Valentine's Day, I bought a new house – I did everything you have been trying to do with Marcus, to trap him over the past 8 years, in less than 3 months; I did it all – guess that is karma for you." Aubrielle snaps at her, picking up her stuff and tries to walk away again.

"What the fuck does karma have to do with this?" Shavon asks confused.

"You stole Marcus from me, you were second – you got him because you deceived him and he knows exactly the disgusting HO you are, he never wanted you, and that is why both of you still only pretend to be together today. I want nothing to do with you – stay the fuck away from me, my kids, and my family. oh p.s. I'm getting married too – fuck u" Aubrielle yells at the top of her lungs, she doesn't know where this rage came from but she does know that if feels better than sex to tell this bitch exactly what she thinks right now.

"Yea ok your ugly ass bitch, Marcus isn't the only one I fucked. I fucked chance too, and it didn't take long after we meet either, the next day to be exact. Right after he left your ugly ass. His body is fucken amazing, all those tattoos, my favorite one is the one dedicated to his dead mother that takes up his whole back." Shavon yells to her back, and make sure she hits her back just as hard and with as much detail as she can.

Aubrielle keeps walking into the building, pretending that she didn't just hear every word of that, but sadly she did. She tries to go to work and act like everything is ok, but it is far from it. Shavon is still in the parking lot, she is enraged she take the bat Marcus keeps in her car and smash every window of Aubrielle truck, then takes a screwdriver and "keys" Aubrielle's car, writing words like ugly and bitch on it, other employees see what she is doing and runs to get security as she pulls a knife out and slashed her tires. The whole incident is caught on camera; she gets arrested and fired immediately for destruction of property and vandalism. Aubrielle's supervisor comes and finds her in with one of the patients, she asks Aubrielle to come with her, she follows her into an empty room, where her boss, Kim Rivers, tells here what just happened. Aubrielle is shaken like crazy and has the sharpest pain in her stomach; she grabs her stomach and screams "my babies." Her boss calls for a doctor, and they admit her to the hospital to check her. They doctor tells her that her blood pressure is throw the roof and she need to remove stress from her life if she wants to have these babies. Her boss suggests that she takes off, for a few days to come down, and rest. She then goes and calls Annelise to come pick Aubrielle up, she informs her of everything she knows, which was only that Shavon destroyed her car and she was in the hospital because of the babies. She didn't know the exchange that took place. Annelise drops the kids off with her mother and runs up to the hospital, as she parks, she sees the police tow truck taking Aubrielle' struck away. Really panicked now, she runs into the hospital to find her sister.

"You ok, are the babies ok?" Annelise ask her, but she can only cry, so she nods yes. Her sister hugs for a few minutes and lets her get it out, gets the details from the doctor on her condition and instructions to keep her and babies ok, and then takes her home.

"Do you want to talk about it? Annelise asks her, Aubrielle purges everything that happened, then remembers her family didn't know anything that happened at momma Shaw's house or Chances past, until know, somehow all that came out to, because the night that Shavon is saying that they fucked was the night a momma Shaw's house when she found out that he was on parole, they fought, he left – that was the first time since they meet that he left her, and that they didn't spend the night together. I keep holding his mother's murder against him too, like that could be me and the babies, but truth is after the way Shavon just acting, you know what can happen and by who."

"Brie, I don't think he would do that. That he would be with her" Annelise says

"That is the thing with Chance all the not possible can be possible- it is the uncertainty of things that piss me off. I don't know what to believe. She knew his body is tattoos, I don't even know if you know. He has a huge cross on his back, it takes up his whole back and it says Joanna across it with angel wings and a halo, she knew it – she said" it was her favorite, the tattoo on his back, dedicated to his mother." Aubrielle, cries, listen to her sister and the details enrage Annelise.

"I have to get the kids from mom, I told her I went to pick you up because you got sick at work and didn't want to drive- I know you don't want to deal, but I am going to drop you off and get them, but I am going to find out what the deal is – can you watch the kids for a minute, I'll bring McDonalds and movies they will be good." She says Aubrielle knows her sister is boiling mad right now, she never lets her kids eat that crap, and she is the one with the balls in the family. Plus, she doesn't want to deal with Chance, so she nods in agreement as they pull up in her driveway.

She gets out and walks up to the door, as Annelise pulls off in a hurry tires shrieking and all. When she walks in, she smells chances cologne, and misses him. Is pissed that her and Chance will now get into another fight, another doubt, more bullshit and drama. It becomes clear why Aubrielle never cared if she was with someone. She never needed anyone to define her, she was independent and strong but most of all content and at peace in her life, until now, until she made the mistake and didn't follow her gut feeling the first time she saw Chance.

She just realized why she kept denying him in the beginning, she felt the trouble that radiated off his skin and know he was a bad boy and was going to bring nothing but hurt to her.

She jumps in the shower, and puts her comfy pajamas on, as she comes back downstairs with her favorite blanket to lie on the new velvet couch, Annelise is back with the kids. She makes all of them sit at the table and feeds them, while she gives auntie Brie, Avanti, and his bottle. As the kids eat, she sets up the pack-n-play next to the couch for the baby and set up the DVD~ she told the kids that Brie, was sick, that the baby was making her tired. So, GG, little miss fixes it, suggests that they should watch CARS, then FINDING NEMO because they were Brie's favorite Disney movies. When she is done setting everything up, she washes the kid's hands and reminds them to be on their best behavior, listen and help auntie. They agree, and she leaves. The kids climb on the couch with her and watch the movies until before long they are all asleep.

Annelise went to the lot, Chance and Javier were both working at 10am today, and neither of them knows what happen with Aubrielle yet, it is now close to one.

"Hello, Dexter. How are you doing? Annelise asks, as Dexter blushed, her was always in love with her.

"Hey luv, what brings you here?" Dexter responses

"I was looking for my husband and brother in law?" Annelise replies.

"Oh, they just went across the street for lunch." Dexter said pointing to the deli. Annelise see them walking into the deli.

"Thanks Dexter!" Annelise says as she drives away.

She walks into the deli and Javier spots her right away "hey beautiful, this is a surprise, what are you doing here?" Javier says excited.

She looks at chance "we need to talk now! Outside." She walks back outside, as Javier and chance look at each other "I think I am scared." Chance says "yup, you need to be bro!" Javier says

They walk outside to the picnic table that Annelise is sitting at, far away from the other tables, although it seems like the lunch crowd has passed since no one is eating outside. The men sit at the table Javier sits next to Annelise and kiss her cheek.

"Where are my babies?" Javier's asks as he looks around, as her eyes stay on Chance she replies, "with my sister."

"Oh, Ang is out, is everything ok, it's unlike her to be off during the week." Javier states.

"Ang is at work; they are with Brie!" she says directly at Chance.

"What?" they say together "Brie is at work." Chances correct her.

"No, she is at home, her boss called me to come get her from work, as she could not work today." She corrects him back. Chance jumps up to leave, to go home to her.

"Sit the fuck down chance- I am not down with you." Annelise snaps. Javier looks at chance, mortified so he knows this is serious, and complies.

"Babe, calm down – what happen." Javier tries to calm the situation.

"Brie went to work, when she pulled in the parking lot her and Shavon got into a heat argument, Shavon was being her normal jealous nosey self, she was pissed when she Brie's truck. Aubrielle said that she lost it, which since we all know Brie, we should know how upset she is because she does not do that, and she was screaming at Shavon to stay away from her, that she knew about Marcus, things really escalated then, right before she fucked up Brie's new truck, managed to get herself arrested and fired, Shavon told Brie that Marcus was not the only one she fucked." Annelise said

"What – where is she – is she ok?? I have to go to her." Chance says, as he stands up.

"Chance sits the fuck down and do not get up again." She snaps

"Lee, why are you talking to me, what did I do?" Chances say puzzled.

"Wait, she said that she fucked Chance." Javier asked.

"Yes, she described his body and tattoos to drive the point home. It put Brie in the hospital, they admitted her for fear of her having a miscarriage from all the stress, her blood pressure was through the roof. They sent her home when things were ok, but want her to avoid stress, and put her on bed rest. Which brings me to you- Chance you turned my sister's life upside down, she has cried more in the past week than in her entire life – and it is not the pregnancies, she told me everything, which now makes sense to what Angelina was telling me. You are to stay the fuck away from my sister." Annelise demands, Javier interjects- "babe, stop this is between them, she is carrying his kids, let them work it out."

"Lee, I don't know what you are talking about with Angelina, or Shavon, but Brie and I are together, we are having twins and I love her more than anything. I am sorry for everything that has happened, but I love her, I will not stay away from her, we will get through this. I never fucken touched that ho" Chances says, feeling defeated and hopeless.

"Angelina said that Demetrius knew about your drug dealing and had a huge file on you, he tried to show her, but she refused, but I won't." Annelise says, as she kisses her husband and walks away.

"Son, what the fuck?" Javier says – "do you fuck her?"

"no." Chances say looking sad and like he his lying

"Chance, really, you did nothing with that girl." Javier asks again

"Remember the other day when I told you what happened the first time, we had dinner at momma's house. With my P.O. and all, {Javier is shaking his head yes} when I left her that night I went home and talked to momma for a while, then tried to go to bed, but I could sleep, I just kept tossing and turning, I did go back to Brie's like I said I did, but I get there at 3 am, I bought her ginger ale and crackers. She was still in the bathroom, the door was locked, so I figured I would go work out until she had to go to work, so I went to the gym. The gym was empty, I had a great workout and when I finished Shavon came in – I didn't even know she went there, but then again it was my first workout in a minute at the gym, I have been doing them at home so I can be with Brie since we first got together. I didn't even recognize her, because I didn't pay attention to her that day, I met her, she stops me and said hello, I said hey, she said you don't remember me? I said no. she said that no nice to insult your so-called girl's best friend. Then it came back to me, I correct her – she is my girl, there is nothing so called about it, unlike her friend's ship, now excuse me I have to go." I walked passed her and took my shirt off to hurry and shower and change to get back to Brie, I thought I lost her when I went in the Men's locker room, but son she followed me in the shower, I turned around and she was there, she tried to suck my joint, I lost my head of a second, she got it in her mouth, she was horrible, but I let her suck it, then reality came back nothing else happened – I told her to get the fuck out." Chance explains.

"Dam man. I know for a white chick she can't suck shit, from what people said in high school. What are you going to do?" Javier replies

"What do I do? Have you ever dipped out of your marriage?" chances ask

"Yes and no – not since we have been married but when we were dating. You should do the only thing you can LIE. Tell her everything other than she got your dick in her mouth. "Javier advises Chance shakes he head in agreement.

Chance pulls out his phone to call Brie, but he keeps getting an error message, he then tries from Javier

Phone, and gets the same message. So, they decided to finish up work quick and leave telling Dexter there is a family emergency.

After Aubrielle wakes up from her nap with the kids, she changes her phone number. They have not hooked up the house phone; they felt it was not needed since they both had cells. Aubrielle check her email, and there is a message from Marcus.

"Hey baby doll, I need to talk to you please call me ASAP! It is urgent, and yes, it is about Shavon, but not what you think - please call me."

She gets goosebumps, she used to love when he called her that, then wonders if he calls ho bag that. She picks up the phone and calls him without hesitation, to her surprise.

"Marcus here." He answers on the first ring, which surprised her because he never answered blocked calls.

"Hey, it's me." She says shyly.

"Thank god you called me; I have been blowing up your phone but kept getting an error message." Marcus says

"I changed my number today." She tells him, he was shocked she had that same number since high school.

"Brie, I need to see you." He pleads.

"For what – I don't want to see that bitch." She snaps

"I don't either, I want to see you – just me. Where are you" Marcus says

"At home." She says

"No, I went by your apartment." He confesses.

"I don't live there anymore; I live on emery way." She says, confess she doesn't know why she just told him that.

"Can I come through?' he asks

"yup." She said she wants to know what he wants; it has been years since they spoke about anything of importance or personal, and she needs a friend. Ten minutes later he is there.

She is at the door before he knocks, the kids are still sleeping and she don't want to deal with them, and she feels bad about it, but she is drained.

"Hey, my baby doll." Marcus says with a huge smile, as he goes to her for a hug.

"Hey, do you mind if we set out here, Annelise babies are asleep and I just can't deal right now, I don't want them to get up." She confesses.

"Of course, I had to come see you." He replies

"I guess you heard," she asks, and he replies "yea I ran into Wally today and he told me you never knew about Shavon knowing we were dating, I always wondered why you to remained friend. It makes sense that you didn't know, but I felt that I had to come to tell talk to you about what happen." Marcus explains, Aubrielle is so confessed right now.

'so, you not here about today and everything that happened?" Aubrielle asks

"No, why what happen today?" Marcus asks

This has been a moment she has waited for, deep down inside for a long time. She begins by asking Marcus what the deal is with Shavon."

"Nothing, she is just around, I can't get rid of her." He says

"Is that what you want, because I can give you all the info you need to do just that, which will lead to today." She tells him

"Please do! I can't take her no more." Her urges her.

"But that makes no sense you two just went on a vacation together." She said

"no, I caught her telling her cousin Josie how she wanted to fuck this cat they call chance she just meets, and we fought, I left to go play a game, she followed me – we fought again – I told him to go home because she had to pack and get the fuck out before I returned, I just got back and ran into Wally and went to holla at you before I have to go home and deal with her." Marcus replies. Aubrielle cries knowing it is true for sure no, even if chance didn't want to Shavon don't take no for an answer. She won't stop until something happens. Marcus moves over holding her to comfort her. She begins at the beginning.

"Chance is my man, we just moved her and I am pregnant with twins, there has been so much going on and on top of it she told me this am she did fuck him, and that is just the tip of it what is going on, and what I have to tell you.' She tells him.

"I am sorry I never acted like I cared about you, I was young and felt like I didn't fit into your fabulous life." She says

"I wish you saw what I see, you are amazing, you have a huge heart, and you're real. In a world of fake ass people, you are real." Marcus said

"Yea I hear that a lot, sad no one else can be. well present company excluded. You always kept it 100%" she said

"Can you tell me know what happen and why your so upset." He requests

She finds comfort in him, they used to talk a lot, and she forgot how much she missed his raw bluntness, and his sweetness, at the same time. He is very religious and encouraging as well. Before she knows it, she tells him everything from beginning to end about chance and about Shavon. It was like a 3-hour conversation in one long breathes. Marcus can clearly careless about Shavon; all he keeps asking her is about her.

"You haven't said anything about that bitch." She says

"I am happy she is in jail, and fired, and thankful to you for the rest of the info so I can finally get rid of her. She is crazy jealous of you; she has always been. I think that is why she lost it today." Marcus says

"Why do you think that- she is jealous?" She asks

"Because she knew you were always my number one, and that I want to be with you. Full disclosure I even called her your name a couple of times, a few times during sex and anytime she did something sweet that was out of her character but was yours. It was funny to me, because it was an accident, but fun throwing it in her face at the same time. Every time we fought, she would try to so something sweet, so I knew she was talking to you, and that was your idea." Marcus tells her "It is still true now, I'm sorry that it is too late, and that you really moved on." He says sadly. "Are your happy Brie?" He asks.

"I don't know, anymore." She replies.

"No matter what, know I love you and I am here for you. "Marcus confesses

"Marcus, tell me what to do?" she pleads

"I wish I could Brie, but if I was too, I would be selfish in my response, I don't want you with anyone else just me. To me your place is with me, I know that now, I think we needed a moment to grow up and see what else was out there. I was hoping to take you away today, make you my girl again. I know you're in a situation, and I respect that and that you must deal with it. So, if I must fall back and wait then I will. But I will remain your friend and like I said I'm here for you and love you. I will finish with this, you deserve better Brie, someone to give you the world, not turn it upside down." just then Annelise pulls up; Chance and Javier are right behind her. Annelise looks pissed, she stopped at the food store and got some things for Brie, since they didn't have much food, so it gave them a Chance to catch up to her, Javier also came back because his family was there, and he knew Chance need a wingman right now, they became close, and he knows the Miakova girls were not easy to deal with.

Chance is pissed that this dude is at their house and has his arm around Brie. Annelise is happy about both things Chance is pissed about, and Javier braces himself.

Annelise goes running over to Marcus, she always liked him. She gives him a huge hug, "hey kiddo" he says just like old times.

"What up man. I haven't seen you guys in a minute congrats on Avanti – glad to see you're taking care of my girls." Marcus says to Javier as they shake hands.

Chance glares at him, Marcus glares back, Aubrielle swallows hard as she can see the mounting tension.

Marcus looks at Brie, he sees every emotion pass through her eyes and tries to defuse it "ok, baby doll, I'm going to head out, like I said I saw you sitting her as I passed by, and waited to check on you. I will replace your truck, or pay for the damages, let me know when they finish everything. If you need anything else let me know – you know, I'm here for you."

"if the rest of you will excuses me, I have some trash to put out of my house, Chance you have an amazing woman, no one compares to her." Marcus says and hugs Brie, and Annelise, before he walks off.

"Thank you, I'll be in touch." Aubrielle responses, Marcus winks at her.

Chapter 12

Marcus just left, Annelise, Javier and kids leave right after him. Annelise didn't want to go, but Javier makes her so Chance and Brie can work things out. Chance doesn't know what to do, but then again neither do Aubrielle. She just goes back to the couch, to lie down. She doesn't know that Annelise confronted him because Javier pulled her away before she could tell her details.

Chance begins to put the stuff away that Annelise brought and make dinner. Aubrielle falls asleep, before long a couple of hours pass when she finally wakes up, Chance is sitting with her on the couch rubbing her belly, talking to his babies. Aubrielle is annoyed that again she feels hurt and betrayed all while still in love with him, but right now her anger takes over as she throws his hand off her.

"Brie, I never touched her." Chance begins, "Annelise came to the lot and told me what she said to you, she was trying to piss you off." he continued after she looks at him confused.

"You know what the problem is here?" Brie asks him, he shakes his head no, he is confessed that her voice is so calm.

"the problem is me, clearly I have very bad taste in people, since someone I used to call my best friend, and the man that I was in love with and who children I am carrying are both selfish, lying backstabbers and I can't and don't believe either of you." She confesses, Chance is now scared, Aubrielle always curses when she is pissed off- but she didn't, she didn't raise her voice, show emotion, nothing just the emotion of being done. She goes to get up, maybe too fast as she was trying to get away from him. When all the sudden she gets dizzy and sharp pains in her stomach.

"Are you ok?" he asks, getting to his feet to help her. "No, you're going to kill me, or worse our babies with all this crap you have been putting me through since the day I found out I was expecting. Stay away from me." She snaps as she makes her get away. Thinking about what she just said and the pain in chances eyes as she said it, as he turned his head away and looked at the picture of him and his mom standing on the fireplace mantle.

As the doctor's words" you must avoid stress if you want to bring these two-little people in this world." repeated in her head. Somehow, she makes her way in the nursery.

She didn't want a traditional blue and pink nursery, or the standard back up of yellow and green. She decided on a cream, khaki and bronze color, it was sweet, with the perfect combo of feminine and masculine. There is a daybed in there which she manages to make her way too. Thinking how she is going to through the next few months with all this stress, then lets her mind wonder to what it would have been like if she was still with Marcus. She reaches for her phone and texts Marcus." Hi"

Three weeks have passed since, Shavon was arrested. A lot has changed since then. Marcus changed all his numbers, his email address, and blocked her from everything. He had dropped everything of Shavon's off at the goodwill. He sold all the cars, and put the house up for sale, but has already moved out so when she did manage to find a way out of jail, she can't find or contact him. Marcus has managed to keep the media out of it, other than issuing a statement that his engagement has come to an end. He even emptied her bank account to get the money back from the 4 engagement rings. Marcus never proposed her to, she bought the ring herself with his money of course and then she showed up to NBA press conference after one of their winning games, she never attended them, or even his games. So, when Marcus saw her there, he knew something was up. Shavon didn't say much, she didn't have to the 6-karat ring on her hand said enough, neither one of them every confirmed or denied the engagement to the press. Aubrielle was not surprised when Marcus told her this, in one of their many conversations over the past few weeks. When Aubrielle asked her how the proposal went Shavon had no answer. So Aubrielle just figured it was bull shit or forced.

Her parents are finally able to raise her bail and took her daughter back in. this is strongly against both their wishes but without money, and a job to have income she has no choice. When she gets out of jail and goes to her parent's mobile home for the first time in five years since she moved out Shavon is digested at what her life comes too. As she sits there and tries to talk to her mother, when she realizes it is pointless, she was always a bigger fan of Aubrielle that she was of her only daughter Shavon thinks to herself. "I don't understand you von, why is it that you are so determined to make other people miserable, that will never bring you true happiness." She mother says.

"Really, and what do you know about happiness." She snaps. "Sweetheart, I am not the one who lives my life alone. I have a husband and friends, you have no one now, so I suggest that the next time you open your mother you do it with respect." Her mother fires" what the hell is with you, anyway, why are you so evil. You had a great childhood, there was no reason for this, had your father, and me. You were not abused so what the hell is it." But deep down her mother knew, she was an only child, a spoiled bitch. Her father gave her anything she ever wanted; she didn't even have to earn it; her mother did everything for her. She never did a chore; she barely did her homework. If she didn't want to or didn't get it, her mother would do that for her too. They raised her with the false reality that everything is handed to you. Of course, they didn't mean it, they loved her, and she was their only child, they didn't mean for her to turn out this way. Shavon sitting in her mother's double wide listening her mother's words, of why can you be more like Aubrielle, really got to her so, Shavon swore right then and there she will get revenge.

Marcus replaced Aubrielle truck. The one that Shavon fucked up was going to take too long to fix, so he just replaced it and the car seats that Shavon through across the parking lot and were never recovered. Of course, he had to show up chance this was all custom interior, and special rims that were painted to match the burnt orange color of the truck. Marcus made sure it was her favorite color. He also gave Aubrielle $250,000 after many fights about it, he called it a settlement she called it charity. "Brie, this will give you the freedom to stay home and not to have to go back to work, so you can avoid the stress and keep the three of you healthy. Please no one knows where Shavon is, but she knows where you work, I don't want you to go back there." He confesses.

Aubrielle finally agreed, this money can be stretched far, since chance paid for the house in cash, they didn't have a mortgage. Now, her truck was paid off thanks also to Marcus, and Chance didn't have a car note either, so their bills were limited. So, not to cause problems he had his attorney send it so it was professional, and chance couldn't say much. However, before they moved in the house, she created a budget of all their bills, so every month they both knew that they had to make at least $1500 to cover the bills, food and anything that may come up, Chance has been bringing home that if not more even though the lot is slow.

Chance, and Brie are still together, if that is what you want to call it. They still live together, but they only speak when they must, they have sex because she can't control the rage with the pregnancy, but she sleeps in the master bedroom, and he will fall asleep on the couch or in the other room so to give her space.

Chapter 13

Shavon makes her first public appearance, since her arrest, it's been 4 months. She shows up at the lot, in a skimpy tight dress, with an obvious baby bump. She was so skinny if she swelled a pee you would see it. Chance is at the lot alone today. Javier took off because Annelise was sick with the flu and he need to take care of the kids. Dexter, and the other salesman, NY 'Aire went to the auction to get new cars for the lot. Shavon new chances were working there, because her cousin Josie just bought a car from the dealership. When she was there Javier sold her the car, but every time he spoke to chance, he called him his bro. so finally she asked why, and Javier said that is Brie's man. Of course, she went running back and ran her mouth to Shavon.

"Hey lover." She says to chance

"Shavon I am not your lover, unless you're buying a car you need to leave." He snaps

"I am not here to give you my money; I am here to get it." She says with a chuckle, only worthy of the evil stepmother in Cinderella.

"Wow, jail thought you to have jokes." He says

"Yea, speaking of that I am surprise you let your baby's mother stay in jail. She says as she rubs her belly.

"Bitch you lost your mind. I would never let a ho like you get pregnant by me, and we never fucked so get the fuck out of here, there is no way that brat is mine." Chance says confidently.

"I guess your mother didn't tell you about the birds and the bees before she passed away, you need to fuck, and you just need the seed." She says

"Bitch, you ever bring my mother's name up again and you will be picking up your mouth off the floor." He says with fire – "you don't fuck you don't get seed."

"Really, because as I remember it, your seed was all over my mouth when you bust that nut, I sucked out of you, and I bottled it up and used it when the time was right, presto baby and baby daddy." She says pointing at him.

"You, fucken evil whore. I want a DNA test." Chance says.

"I have a few tests tomorrow, to make sure there no issues they can do a DNA test, you can take me to it." She says.

"Fuck I will, I am not taking you anywhere." He replies.

"well, meet me there, then after words we can talk terms – and so there is no doubt let me tell you in advance, if you don't meet them, I will tell." Shavon says "tomorrow Dr. Mandina 2pm "she finishes.

"What – no that is Brie's doctor." He says afraid.

"I know – tomorrow at 2 or else" she says. She leaves the parking lot just as Dexter, and NY 'Aire come back from the auction. After going over the inventory of the 20 new cars that they just got, Chance leaves for the day, he's shift has ended, and not a moment too soon. He is freaking out to say the least. He doesn't know what to do, where to go or who to talk to. He calls Javier but he is knee deep in throw up, since all 4 kids are sick now too. He goes to Momma Shaw's house, but she is at work, so are Blue and Dizzy. Mariah and Xavier are at school and too young to talk to about this. He and his boys are still tight, although their lives are going into a different direction, since all three are in serious relationships now. Chance lies down on his old bed; he has the worse migraine and knows since Aubrielle is keeping her distance she won't be looking for him. It is 6pm before he knows it; he has been asleep for the past three hours, when he wakes up to his phone ringing.

"Where are you?" Brie asks, "I thought you got off at three"

"I did, I am at Momma's house" he says.

"Yea, right you sound like you just woke up, and no one is there until after 7 in the evening, every day." She says.

"Brie, I am at momma house, I am waiting for Blue." He responses sincerely.

"You are fucken full of shit, Blue is here, so fuck you and that bitch your with." She says and slams the phone down. He takes a picture of him lying in bed and sends it to her. It was the suit and tie he had on this morning when he left, but whatever so what he is there now, it doesn't mean he was there all this time. She ignores it. Blue calls him in front of her "what up, man I got your text you said you need to talk, and it was urgent, so I came right to your house when I got off." Blue says.

"I am momma's, come here." Chance says.

"I'm sorry brie that I bothered you, I'll let myself out." Blue says

"Wait, what is going on? You said it was urgent- where are you going? Brie pleads.

"I don't know what is going on, he wants me to meet him at home, so I'm going there." Blue answers, then continues "he loves you; I know for the past few months things have been, shall I say cold between you too. I know he hates it and it is getting to him especially with you over 7 months now, he doesn't want you to hate each other when the babies are here, or them to see their mom and dad like this."

"Blue, I hate this, but I didn't do it. Every time I let him back in something huge and that hurts me to my core happens. I love him, but I don't want the bull shit that comes with him. "She says crying, Blue hugs her, and tell her "no one is perfect Brie, but he is trying to be what you want." He kisses her forehead and lets himself out.

When Blue gets to the house chance is still laying down in his old room. Chance sees him and begins to cry, like he did the day his mother died. Blue goes over to him and hugs. he stops and then chance tells him what happened today. "Son, what the fuck is this bitch's problem." Blue asks

"I don't know, but what the fuck do I do, it's already bad enough that I have gone back to hustling myself to make ends meet, and now this shit." Chances says

"Yea, I guess Brie being out for this month has hit hard, I know she can't go back, she is huge and uncomfortable, she could barely move just now." Blue says.

"Why don't you finally rent out the apartment for income?" Blue asks

"To whom? She doesn't want a chick there, she said so I can sneak over there and fuck the bitch, I just can't win, whatever I say she thinks I'm up to something." Chance said.

"Well, Momma is losing this house, the landlord has sold it, we are all looking now!" Blue says.

"What- why didn't you say again!" chance says "you guys are moving in- I don't want to her another word- tell momma to pack up. I'm going home to tell Brie."

"Wait- she heard us on the phone when I told you, you said it was urgent." Blue starts to say

"Momma's losing her house that is urgent- love you bro. I'll hit you up later." They hugged and chance races home to talk to Brie.

Chance walks in the door, Brie is in the bathtub soaking. She is in there a lot lately, the water makes the pain go away, and her body feels light. Chance goes in the bathroom.

"Hi sweet pea." He says as he kisses her forehead, and then the little bit of her belly that is sticking out of water. "Can we talk for a second?" He asks. She nods, he sees she has been crying. Brie went from being upset, to now pissed off, it has been a while since he greeted her like that, but it is all my fault for that she keeps thing. Which is her fault, she won't let him near her.

"I wasn't with someone else, after work I went to Momma's house, to talk to Blue because I found out that Momma lost her house. The landlord sold it; they need to move." Chance tells her, she looks just as shocked as he did.

"Why didn't they say anything?" she asks

"I think because we are not on the best of terms, and with the babies coming they or she didn't want to burden us." he confides "Brie I was thinking that." He starts to say

"Why don't they move into the apartment, we can use the help" she suggest, as she stands to get out of the tub, he takes her arm to help her over the tub, and then stands back not to overcrowded her, he doesn't want to piss her off and this is a very serious topic ~ it's his family they are talking about. Just then he sees her, for the first time in months he sees her, and the babies.

"You don't mind, I was thinking the same thing, but I wanted to run it past you. "Chance says

She says "of course, they are family. I will not let them live on the streets, plus we are having twins I am going to need help, and with me not working we need the income – wait are they going to pay rent – I mean of course we are going be easy but still say $1000. So, then we only should come up with a little bit of the money for our bills, because our expenses for these two are going to be a lot. She says, as she is trying to dry off her body as best she can with her back towards Chance, when she finally looks up in the mirrors her bathroom wall is covered in from floor to ceiling, she gets annoyed with the look on his face only to realize again she is wrong. "Hello, why are you staring at me like that – shit I know I am ugly and fat but really chance." Brie says, as she gets choked up like she is about to cry. Trying to quickly cover herself up.

"You are far from ugly or fat. You look beautiful – I just haven't seen your belly or you in a while. I can see them moving inside you, and the more you talk the more they do it, it's like they love your voice. It's beautiful." Chance says emotional.

"Why are you crying?" Brie asks concerned, and scared she has never seen him cry, let alone this bad.

"I love you; I love our babies. I don't want to lose you, or them. I want you back. It is the holidays. Thanksgiving was horrible; we didn't even talk to each other or really see each other. I was at mommas and you were at your moms. I know it's hard for you to move around and you're not comfortable. I also know that your parents must be questioning you. I don't want Christmas like that, and the doc said you were not going to carry until your due date. You can go into labor at any time Brie. I am sorry- please can we please be together again. I don't want to live my life separate from you under the same roof or not. "Chances rumbles off through his tears, reach out touching her belly. Which the second he does the babies go crazy doing all kinds of flips. He takes the towel from her and helps dry her skin again. Thinking of her babies, and the life and family she wants them to have, as well as being brought up in a 2-parent household, she decides to try again.

"James" she says.

Shocked she called him that, it is rare "yes, baby."

"I love you" she confesses, chance kisses her "can we go to bed?" She asks.

"Yea, we can go to sleep." He says.

"I don't want to sleep." She says as she takes his hand and leads to him to the bed.

She pushes him down on the bed, as they kiss, she undoes the buttons on his shirt, then his pants. She sticks her hand down his pants and pulls out his dick. She gets more excited, knowing just how much chance loves when she sucks on him. Nothing turns him on more; he even used to suck his thumb when she gave him head, or after he stepped inside of her if they had not had sex in a few days. It was like he was a little boy who just came home, she loved it.

But today, the moment her lips touch his manhood, he told her to stop. When he closed his eyes, he would remember the day at the gym with Shavon and then today on the lot. He could get rid of that hunting image of Shavon and her pregnant belly.

"What is wrong?" she asks, paranoid that he did fuck someone else today or that he don't want her.

"It has been a minute, you know how much I love when you give me head, and as much as I miss and want you, I won't last long, and I want to make love to you." He says, then begging to kiss her slowing moving her on the bed, he lays her on her side, and lays behind her, kissing all over her neck, shoulders, and lips – the very thing he knows drives her crazy and they make love until morning.

The next day he goes to meet up with Shavon for the appointment. She had A Prenatal DNA paternity test - DNA test during pregnancy must be performed by obtaining either a small sample of the placenta (i.e., chorionic villus sampling), or a sample of amniotic fluid that bathes the baby (i.e., amniocentesis) in this case they used the fluid. The whole time they were the Dr. Mandina keep staring at chance, like she knew him but didn't know from where. Chance of course that is was because she knew from where. After they took the samples from both Chance, and Shavon the doctor told them that it will be a few weeks before they had the results. And that they will contact them with the results. After the appointment, Chance told her that he wasn't taking to her about shit let alone terms until they knew for sure and sent her on her way, he stayed back to catch up with the doctor.

"Dr. Mandina, I am sorry may I have a word with you." Chances asks

"Yes, of course, I must say you look so familiar, but I can't think of where, do I know you?" she asks

"Yes, my girl is your patient we are expected." Chance responses

"That is funny; I know that I didn't lose my memory in the ten minutes after your exam." Dr. Mandina says thinking he is speaking of Shavon.

"No, doc. My girl Aubrielle, we are having twins." Chance says sadly.

"Oh my, I see." Dr. says shaking her head

"It is not what you think, please let me explain. First please know that Brie doesn't know anything about this, I never had sex with Shavon." Chance says

"I'm sorry I don't understand." The doctor says

Chance tells her what had happened, at the gym. "I mean I didn't stay to see if she had a mouth full or even a drop, I know it takes one sperm to make a baby. But could this baby really be mine?" chance asks

"It depends, like you said you did ejaculate, which is sperm and you only need one. So, I am afraid I cannot speculate, just as you can't. I can rush the order though, so we can find out the results as quick as we can." Doctor says.

"Ok, please I know doctor- patient privileges but I also know you and brie are friends. Please don't say anything to her." Chances begs

"Know worries there under the HIPAA laws, I can't, and yes I am her friend, and think very highly of her, but I don't want to be one to tell her this. "She says

"Ok, I'll see you on Friday for Brie's appointment – and thank you." He says

"James, if I may just say this doesn't surprise me about Shavon, she is evil, and always seemed to be jealous of Brie, either way you need to make this right, and stay away from her." Doc says

"Yes, I will. I promise that." Chance says.

Chance leaves, and then goes to meet with his dealer. He gave Lawrence "lucky" Ross $20.000 in cash last week that he has been waiting on a return from. Lucky is nowhere to be found. Chance waits for three hours for him at their meetup stop, but he never shows. Chance is tight, that was the last of his money his mom left, that he had in cash, he had made investments with most of it and can't withdraw the money without heavy penalties, and then he bought the house. He starts to look around for him, questioning known fens, and other dealers, who were on the nickel and dime level. Chance finally tracks him down at some crack head motel, three towns over. Someone bet this boys ass. Chance questions him

"Lucky, what the fuck happens to you" chance asks

"Man, after you dropped the money off, I got robbed. They saw us; they see you give me the money." Lucky responses.

"Who?" chance says

"Izzy and his boys. They took the money. They said if you had a problem that you can come see them, but said to warn you that this time, it wasn't going to be your mommy, it was going to be you."

"What do you mean, not my mom?" Chance asks he scratches his head.

"you, man you have not heard – aww fuck man – I don't want to be the one to tell you this. Izzy claims he shot your mom. "he says. Chances memories flash before his eyes.

Isaac "Izzy" Brown and chance were friends in grade school. Izzy was a star football player. He had several colleges looking at him. Chance and he became enemies because in the 11th grade they were playing around, when Chance tripped Izzy, breaking his arm and waist in 3 places. The bills from the surgery, they had to perform to line the arm up correctly again, put Izzy's mom is serious debt. Shortly after breaking his arm, his mother was diagnosed with breast cancer. His family did not have health insurance. After their father left them, his mom worked a bunch of part time fast food jobs, she couldn't even get a full 40-hour work week let alone insurance. His father worked jobs off the books, so he didn't have to pay child support. Izzy's mom, Sarah began to sell drugs for the same guy Chance did. Izzy thought that Chance knew, but Chance found out only after his mom got in deep, she was not just selling drugs but using and selling herself too. She was doing everything and anything to make money to pay for her cancer treatments, Izzy's arm, and to support her and her 5 children in general. She ended up getting so high on heroin she jumped in front of a moving Mac Truck. Which was her 3 attempts at suicide. The first time she was in a car, and hooked up the exhausted hose wrong, so the carbon monoxide gas didn't kill her, the second time she slit her wrists in the bathtub Izzy found her and got her help. He swears she was pushed, but everyone knew that it was because he just didn't want to face the truth. He never went to college or played in the NFL as he dreamed. He stayed to take care of his little sisters, working any dead-end job he could. He even dropped

107

out of high school, and he began to hustle too. Before long he was one of the most notorious dealers in the area, and to say that he was ruthless was the truth, everyone feared him. Although he stayed low-key everyone knew his name wither, they did drugs, sold them or just lived in the area. He always blamed Chance for everything that happen, because as far as he knew his mom became the hot mess the day, he broke his arm, but truth is she was like that way before. All of it drugs, selling herself, even in and out of jail, and that was the real reason his father left. Izzy said, "since that mother fucker took my moms, I'm going to take his and make him suffer like me and my little sisters do every day."

Chapter 14

Chance head is swirling he doesn't know what to do anymore. He has lost control of everything around him, and when Aubrielle founds out about Sharon's baby and now this, it is going to be game over for him. He thinks to himself as he walks around the marina, he took Aubrielle on their first date. He's thoughts are interrupted when someone taps his shoulder, it is Demetrius. "We need to talk." He tells chance.

"Why, so you can try to out me like that again in front Aubrielle and her family. What the hell was that shit." Chance snaps.

"I saw your picture earlier that day, when your file was dropped on my desk, I had no idea who you were until then, then after reading your file and dealing with your case all day, I go to my girls families house for dinner, and sit across the table from you. You would be like what the fuck too!" Demetrius informs him.

"Oh, right the file you try to give Angie. What the fuck is it your business anyway." Chance says

"I don't know how to say this but, your lives on the line. Which means so is Aubrielle, the babies and the rest of the family. An informant that was arrested told a detective that that this guy knows as Izzy is after you. You are putting my girl and her family, and your life in the line of fire – damn straight it is my business. Not to mention it's my job, you really pissed this guy off, he, is taken credit for the murder of your mother, we have some evidence, the gun for one but we need it one tape – when the detective in charge of this was going to ask you to wear the wire – I told him I would – I went to Ang to help me convince you to keep Aubrielle and the rest of her family safe – but she wouldn't listen to any of it." Demetrius tries to explain as Chance looks at him like he is stupid.

"I am not wearing shit." Chance snaps, just as he sees one of Izzy's boys ride by. "Man, I got to go." Chance says as he hurries away, not knowing if Izzy's man, Poochie, knows who Demetrius is, or why he could possibly be meeting with Chance, even if he doesn't know that suit, tie and briefcase say that the is on the opposite side of the law than chance and Izzy.

Later that afternoon, Chance and Aubrielle go to the doctors for a check-up. After they go into the exam room, the doctor comes in. Aubrielle and Chance were doing well again, and so into each other and their babies they didn't even notice that Shavon's cousin Josie was working there now. Shortly after the exam began, Josie busts into the room and says

"Doctor, I was told to bring you this immediately." Josie says.

"I am in the middle of an exam." The doctor corrects her.

"I know, but this the results of the tests you ordered, regarding this couple." Josie says

Aubrielle is pissed, she knows who Josie is but Chance is just sitting there looking stupid.

"Ok" the doctor says, looking confused when she read the results realizing that it is the DNA results for Chance and Shavon. "Put this in my office." She directs Josie.

"What, what is wrong with my babies." Aubrielle cries out, as she tries to read the expression on the doctor face, but can't as it is a mixture of confusion, and anger.

"Nothing is wrong with you or the babies Aubrielle." The doctors say trying to inform her.

"But Josie said it was about this couple, meaning me and James. "She cries out

"You know Josie?" the doctor asks, as Josie walks out of the room.

"Yes, her and my ex best friend are cousins – you know Shavon from the hospital. "Aubrielle tells her.

As the doctor and Chance glance at each other, they both sallow hard, with wide eyes.

"Somebody tell me what the fuck is going on." Aubrielle demands.

"I'll leave you two alone." The doctors say." and "yes James it's confirmed"

Chance begins to cry, he cannot stop. Aubrielle doesn't even stop to ask him, she fixes her clothes and walks out of the room and goes to the doctor's office.

"Give me that file." She demands

"I cannot do that – you know that brie. I am so sorry. I don't know why Shavon is doing this." She says

"Why Shavon is doing what?" Brie asks

"I thought he told you, Shavon is a patient of mine. She is expecting." She states, as Aubrielle looks at her confused.

"Are you telling me that James and Shavon are having a child together?" She finally says

"I'm sorry Brie, I can't tell you. You know that." She says, as she hugs her.

"But you said it was confirmed to him in the room, you were confirming he is the father." She begs Doctor Mandina, as Chance walks in the room, hearing Aubrille's question, Doctor Mandina looks at Chances, Aubrielle's eyes follow hers to Chance and shakes his head yes, Aubrielle scream and grabs her stomach in pain. Doctor Mandina must hold

Aubrielle up, and Chance races over to help, Doctor Mandina instructs the nurse to call 911, as Aubrielle has been a high-risk pregnancy from the stress. The thought of this is just too much for Aubrielle to bear, the stress sends her into premature labor, as her water breaks.

Chapter 15

Feeling completely out of it, Aubrielle tries to find the strength to open her eyes. She hears a sweet sound almost humming when she realizes it is her mother calling her name.

"Mom "she tries to call out, but when her mouth open, she is shocked at how dry her mouth is.

"It's okay baby, mommy is here. You just rest." Adrianna reassures her, just as Aubrielle starts to try to remember what happen and figure out where she is. She remembers the sound of the siren from the ambulance. She feels her stomach which is much flatter now and shots up like a rocket, and begins to scream "My babies, where are my babies?" hysterically. No one can control her, the doctor is called and comes in with a sedative to try and help calm her down, there are strangers everywhere fighting to hold her down and she is trying to fight back and screaming for her babies all while looking around for her mother, her babies, sisters or even Chance. The nurse made all of them get out, when she became hysterical. Just as Chance pops into her head, the meds kick in and she is back out.

When the ambulance came to take Aubrielle to the hospital, she was in active labor, their son was already in the birth canal. She gave birth to him in the ambulance loading dock in the parking lot of the hospital, while still in the ambulance. They then rushed her into the operating room for her birth of her daughter, they had to take the little girl via C-section because the baby's heart rate dropped, and she was in distress. The babies were in the NICU. Aubrielle is on a different floor recovering, Chance has been torn between not leaving the babies side or Aubrielle's. He has tried to speak to her family, but they are not speaking to him after what had happen. Momma Shaw has been the mediator through this whole thing. They decided Chance will stay with the babies, because that is what Aubrielle would want, from him not to leave their babies. Adrianna has not left the side of her baby, Aubrielle. Aubrielle and the babies are ok, but not where the doctors think they should be, so they keep saying that they are still fighting.

Whenever Aubrielle's father or sisters come up, her mother goes to check on the babies. Momma Shaw or Blue and Dizzy are often with Chance, but Adrianna is trying to get him while he is alone. Finally let in the afternoon when she goes to check up on them the babies are alone, the nurse tells her Chance just left to go to the bathroom.

Staring at the babies, Adrianna is lost in her own world and barely hears Chance when he returns from the bathroom.

"Aren't they beautiful?" he asks her. "Joanna looks just like my mother, and little Antonio is the clone of Aubrielle's father. He continued.

"yes, they are. I think you and I need to talk." She replies

"I know you have a lot of questions, and so do I. and I don't know how to answer any of them." He says as a shy little boy.

"the truth tries that. "she demands.

At this point Chances doesn't know what she knows and what she doesn't, so he figured that he would start with the Shavon thing and if she wanted to know anything else, she wouldn't be afraid to ask. He tries very hard to explain things to her in a respectful manner, and to give her the details she is looking for without too much detail that crosses the line. This is the woman that he loves mother after all, not one of the boys. He even tells her how she picked Dr. Mandina on purpose knowing Brie went to her, and even how Dr. Mandina heard Shavon tell how she got pregnant on purpose without having sex with James.

Adrianna says, "thank you for your time" and begins to walk away. "Wait" Chance yells.

"Chance I need a moment it processes this story you just told, and I would like to speak with Dr. Mandina she may need you to give permission to give the details she knows. Adrianna informs him.

"Of course. I'll do anything." He says.

"ok, I will set up a meeting for us to see her. Thank you." She finishes the conversation.

Adrianna goes to find Dr. Mandina, they know each other well. When Adrianna approaches Dr. Mandina she has a warm smile on her face, she always liked her. Adrianna quickly explains she would just like her to meet with her and James to get the details worked out but doctor Mandina says in one quick breathe "off the record, I can confirm Shavon is an evil bitch, trying to get to Aubrielle any way she can. I really feel bad for James he really didn't do anything wrong from what I was told by both James and Shavon – I cannot go into details but it is a long complex story and has Shavon's evil ass all over it." That was really all Adrianna needed to know anyway. Just as they end their conversation about the Shavon's pregnancy, the nurse comes over and say Aubrielle is waking up again, both woman rush to her side.

"Mom?" Aubrielle calls out.

"I'm right here honey, just rest and listen to me ok." Adrianna begins, as this time trying to beat her to the punch of asking for the babies. She continues to explain what happen "Hunny, you're in the hospital, Dr. Mandina is right here, the babies and you are okay, but you did give birth. James is with them at the NICU, he hasn't left their side although conflicted to be here with you, but he knows I got you."

Aubrielle just lays in silence as the tears roll down her face, "Shavon's baby" she whispered, her mother holds her a little bit tighter and begins to define chance, Aubrielle doesn't want to hear it, so she just stays silent, thinking her thought to herself. "this bullshit almost really cost her life or her baby's life and they are not out of the clear yet." Hours have passed since Aubrielle has woke up, she hasn't spoken at all other than to ask to see the babies. The doctor gives her approval to do but they must wait for someone from transportation to bring a wheelchair, she doesn't want Aubrielle walking around for her own safety right now.

Adrianna walks next to her daughter as the volunteer for the hospital's transportation department pushes the wheelchair through the long cold smelly hallways of the hospital. Chance has no idea she is even awake, as no one told him. His face lights up like Christmas tree when he sees her, he goes running over to her and tries to hug her.

"Oh, I'm sorry did I invite you to touch me?" she snaps at him in an extremely cold, in a I'm not having it voice.

"Brie. I' Chances searches for the words to fix this

"Let me stop you right there, no words or actions can ever fix what you have done. I am here to see my babies ~ they are mine!!" Aubrielle fires off at him.

Chance doesn't know what to do, so he just simple says "they are waiting for you. thank you, Brie. They are the most beautiful thing I have ever laid eyes on. Thank you for making me a father."

Chance could have not picked a worse time to thank her. "Father – what kind of fucken father are you — you almost killed them, and still could – get away from me and my babies with your bullshit." She screams at him in the hallway. Chance not knowing what to do and feeling defeated he leaves the hospital.

Not sure of what his next move should be, since Momma lost the house and they are in the process of moving into Chance's and Aubrielle' s. Chance goes back to the house and packs up as much as he can of his clothes, and mainly the items he needs for work. And his most prized items the picture of him and his mother that was on the fireplace mantle and a picture of him and Aubrielle that was on the mantle as well, when she was pregnant. He had pictures of the babies first few hours on both his phone and camera that were at Walgreens being printed out. He leaves a note on the counter for Aubrielle.

> *Aubrielle,*
>
> *I am doing as you wish and leaving you be. I will send you money weekly for the household expenses and for the babies. I would like to set up a visitation schedule when you can. My phone as you know will always be on, and I will always be here for the 3 of you.*
>
> *Love you.*

Chances does a final lap around the house to look at everything he has lost. And leaves the house. Only stopping at in the kitchen to leave his house key on the counter, on top of the note he left.

Ginamarie Foceri

As he packs up, he calls to Dexter to let him know he will not be in tomorrow because of the babies and he needed to find a place, Dexter tells him there was an empty space on the lot, that was the old break room. It has a little kitchenette and a bathroom including a shower, and that he could stay there as some former employees once did. The owner feels better when someone is living on the property because they can watch over the lot, and with doing so rent is limited since you are now employed 24 hours a day, 7 days a week. – he bought a cot and a tv. So, he had the basics. And it was tucked away from the world, so he felt safe there.

Chapter 16

Aubrielle is being discharged from the hospital, However the babies must stay until they put more weight on and are strong enough. It's been two days since she saw Chance. She doesn't know how to feel or think about Chance right now, she does feel bad about how she snapped at him but at the same time he put her in a really messed up spot so why should she care. Her main concern was she was leaving the hospital without her babies. She just keeps telling herself that she will deal with chance later tonight when they get home, looking at her watch she starts to pack her bags thinking Chance will be there at any moment to pick her up and take her home.

After she packs her stuff, Aubrielle goes to check on the babies spend time with them before she leaves them there alone. She's with them for a couple of hours and realizes at any second she will have to leave and starts to have a panic attack thinking about it and then to try and calm herself down she begins to talk herself out of it but only adds to it.

"These people are your friends, you have been working here for years, they aren't going to let anything happen to them." She keeps saying repeatedly to herself, looking at all the pictures on the hallway walls, they have outside of the elevators on every floor to give the visitors something to look at, and encourage them to make donations to the hospital. On this wall, it had pictures from the Christmas party 3 years ago. She did not want to go, but Shavon made her and she looks down her panic attack gets worse as she finds the picture of her and Shavon, but this time when she looks at the picture she notices something that she never did notice before. Marcus is in the picture too, and he is staring at her. She begins to wonder way she never noticed it before. She rips the picture off the wall and sees her watch out of the corner of her eye and realizes Chance has been off for hours. She calls him but he doesn't pick up. As she hangs up from Chance, Marcus is calling her name.

"Hey baby doll." He says bending over to kiss her forehead. "I thought I missed you." Marcus has been to the hospital once other time to check on Brie and the babies, but then had to leave town on a business trip. She is looking at him and then the babies and wants to cry because in that very moment the only thing she could think of is how she wished he was the father and was there to take them all home.

"Brie, what's wrong?" he asks.

"I am going home today, and I have to leave the babies, Chance has been off for hours and I can't reach him. "she says in a whisper hoping he didn't really her, as she is embarrassed.

"Well, good thing old Marcus is here to save the day!' Marcus says smiles at her, and then continues with "you know, I will always catch you." She smiles and feels a comfort she hasn't felt in a long time, and never with Chance. Marcus kisses her head again and tell her he wants to see the babies and then gets her bags. After commenting on their beauty, he turns to her and says "I'm going to give you a minute and put this stuff in the car. I'll have the nurse order the wheelchair, so it will be here when I am back." Marcus states to her, as she nods in agreement. AS she in not allowed to walk out of the hospital all patients must be transported in a wheelchair, as it is hospital policy.

Brie goes to her babies, and explain she is leaving but promises to be back first thing in the morning and tells them to be good for the nurse. She hates looking at them in the incubator, and with all the tubes and machines around them. She can't wait until she can touch them and hold them. As she whispers, I love you to Antonio, he smiles, it melts her heart. She goes to Joanna to whisper she loves her too, but after she does say it, an alarm goes off and 3 nurses run in the room, Destiny, and follow nurse and friend, pushes Aubrielle out of the room, "I'm so sorry Brie, you know the drill. Let them work." She informs Brie on the other side of the doors, then closes them and the curtain so she can't see in, as Marcus gets off the elevator, he runs over to, because he hears the alarm and sees all the staff in the room with the babies.

Marcus is holding her as she sobs into his shoulder. "What is happening?" he asked. "My daughter may die" she screams. He hugs her as tight as he can without breaking her and begins to pray out loud. As he does, Aubrielle starts to say the prayer to, she recalls it from a poster they have hanging up in the children's wing of the hospital. Aubrielle used to look at the poster all the time when she worked there and didn't understand how those parents were so strong and had such patience. Never did she think that one day she would be on the other side of that poem as a parent. She can picture it so clearly and continues to say the words with Marcus.

Joanna stopped breathing for about 2 minutes, they don't know if any damage has been done, and if so the extent of it. The doctor informs her it may be years before they see side effects from it. She stops breathing 2 more times throughout the night, but both times they were much quicker than the first. Aubrielle and Marcus are still at the hospital, Destiny brought them a chair and a cot for them to sleep on, they all knew Aubrielle wasn't going anywhere now. She has been blowing up

Chance all night, but he has not picked up or called back. She has called momma, Blue and Dizzy and given them the play by play of what is going on. The boys have gone out a few times to try and find Chance, but he was nowhere to be found. By the morning time, Doctor Mandina, Destiny and Marcus try to convince Aubrielle to go home and get some sleep, that she is no good to anyone especially her babies with the amount of pain she is in and how exhausted she is. Just then her mother comes around the corner she doesn't know what happen with Joanna throughout the night. Marcus fills her in quickly and then her mother demands she goes home and gets some rest and she will call if anything happens. She finishes with "Dear I'll call you if anything happens and Chance can bring you back up." She glares at her mother, when Marcus steps in to save her. "Ms. Adrianna, if anything happens, I will bring her back up, I am not leaving her right now." He says. Her mother than realizes she still has not spoken to him and leaves it alone for now since there is bigger issues.

They pull in the driveway, and Marcus helps Aubrielle out of the truck. As they walk over to the house Blue comes running over. "I'll take it from here." He says with an attitude Aubrielle has never seen before. "Marcus smiles and replies, "I got her- thanks" Blue snaps at her "Brie you're not about to let another man help you in my brother's house, are you?" Marcus looks around to be funny and snaps back "you have no idea what this woman has been through in the last 24 hours. well fuck, the last few months, she damn sure, is not about to be spoken to like that by you." Marcus say standing an inch away from Blue's face. Just as Aubrielle grabs her stomach in pain, Marcus picks her up and tells him to open the door. He brings her in and lays her on the couch. "Can I get you anything, baby doll?" Marcus says, but she shakes her no. Marcus then sees Blue is also shaking his head no. "Look I know that's your brother and you got love for him and feel the need to protect him, I respect it – I get it but his girl just had his babies after finding out his mistress is also pregnant and he is not here to help her get settled at home, he wasn't around when she calls that his daughter is having issues – come one man – get with it." Marcus recaps, as he sits next to Brie rubbing her head like she used to love, again whines pain. She had not been taking her pills because she wanted to be awake during Joanna's struggle to find out what was going on. "Where are your pain meds?" Blue asks. "In the truck still, I'll get your stuff." Marcus says. Blue nods and makes his way to the kitchen to get her some water to take the pills with. Aubrielle just lays there praying this is all a bad dream. Blue goes over to the cabinet to get a glass and is at the fridge filling it up with ice and water from the door when Marcus comes in, and says hey what is this, as he sees the key on the counter. "What the fuck son, your man is a real piece of shit." Marcus says with fire. 'What do you mean Blue questions, as Marcus points to the counter where the note and key are. Both men look at each other after Blue reads it. "Not, a word to Brie" they both say.

Chapter 17

The night Chance left Aubrielle and the babies, after packing up and shopping for his little corner on the lot. He goes to make it homie. Chance has OCD bad, and the place was messy, but he knew he could make it work it had potential. But after cleaning, putting together the cot and cable he had nothing to do and was bored, his mind kept racing. He decided to do something he never did, ever not once since the day of the funeral. He went to his mother's grave. He wanted to talk to her, hold her one more time. He stopped at the liquor store on the corner before the cemetery and grabbed a bottle of Hennessy, and some Dutch master cigars. It's been forever since he got twisted but need this more than life right now. He smokes his blunt and drank his bottle while he sat and talked to his mother about everything that was going on. He cried to her, he cried for her, for Aubrielle and his babies. He begged for her to take him away to be with her. By the time the bottle was empty Chance was to mess up to drive, so he grabbed a blanket out of his car and slept next to his mother for the first time in years.

The next morning, he wakes up to the landscapers cutting the grass in the cemetery, it's far away but it echoes through the tombstones. He tries to stand, and says goodbye to his mother, he promises he will come more often. Chance stumbles to the car, as he is still intoxicated. He starts to drive home, when he gets to the house, he remembers he has no home here anymore, as he doesn't live there anymore. He sees momma Shaw planting flowers by the apartment, he admires her from a distance for a moment and then pulls off. As he pulls off the tires screech, and then momma Shaw realizes he was there. She tries to flag him down, but he does see her. He goes back to the liquor store and gets some more supplies on his way home. For the next few days, he is held up in the apartment drinking and smoking his problems away. Chances phone had died because he forgot to plug it in and really didn't care since he knew Aubrielle wasn't calling anytime soon. He leaves the apartment only to get more supplies. He finally checks his phone and sees all the misses calls from Brie momma and his boys, He hears the message about Joanna and her crisis, Chance doesn't even know what day it is. He showers quickly to wake himself up and to get rid of whatever he can of the liquor coming through his pores, but it does work. He stumbles out to his car and gets behind the wheel, Chance flies in the direction of the hospital, somehow, he manages to get there without hurting himself or anyone else or pulled over since his driving was reckless. When he finally reaches the NICU, he can see Aubrielle, just as he sees Marcus come out of nowhere, to put his arm around, her kissing her forehead. Nothing irks Chance more than when he does that, he knows how a woman buy into that crap, how loving and endearing it is. Chance stumbles walking over to them, tripping on his two feet. When Aubrielle turns and hugs Marcus around his waist, Chance loses it. "Yo, Bitch" he screams, everyone turns around and looks to see what is going on.

Aubrielle looks at him dazed and confused herself, as at first, she doesn't even realize it is him. He looks like he dropped 30 pounds over night, which for him is a lot. Chance was all muscle when they met. He had no body fat at all, and now his face looks so sunk in, has bags under his eyes that almost reach is chin. He has not shaved or got a hair cuts in days, which is also out of character for him. He looks like Skelton and the Wolverine combined. His clothes don't even match. Aubrielle' s heart crumbles when she sees him.

"I want to see my babies alone!!!!!!! I don't want you and your man here – got it!" he snaps. Marcus steps forward like he is about to say something, Aubrielle grabs his shirt and with her entire body pushes him in the opposite direction, they go to the waiting area, and get a cup of coffee. Marcus is mad as hell.

"Brie, I don't give a fuck no one has the right to talk to you like that." He starts. "Please, Marcus don't – leave it be, this is not the time or place and not in front of my babies. I know they are young, but I will not do that in front of them, I don't care how old they are. I will get in that habit and make them thinks it is normal behavior. And look at him. That is not my Chance." Marcus see the way she is looking at him, and the words "my Chance" keeps echoing in his head.

"OH ok, well let me leave you two be then." He says storming out of the hospital, Brie is pissed but can't deal with him being in his feeling right now. She walks over to the babies and Chance. Chance has he head down by Joanna, as he is whispering to her, but Aubrielle can't make out the words. She closes the glass doors behind her, then the curtain to give them some privacy. He is crying, and tears run down her face as she walks over to him, she pushes on his chest to get him to sit up right, as she goes to sit on his lap and comfort him, he pushes her away, hard enough that she falls to the floor. Chance just looks at her, steps over her, and in a voice, she has never heard says "it takes a real ho to go from to another that quickly, have fun bouncing on your new man's dick, don't try to come back to mine." As he walks away, doesn't say anything to the babies, doesn't help her to her feet, he just leaves her.

Momma Shaw comes in the room right after, Aubrielle is sobbing uncontrollably, she is crying so hard she can't catch her breathe or make a sound. And momma just holds her. Aubrielle tells momma what happen. All she can say is you two need time, Aubrielle doesn't want to hear it, just as chance never does.

It's now almost 9 pm and time for them to leave the hospital, as visiting hours are over. Momma Shaw drives home, and the 2 women sit in silence. When they get to the house, they go into their separate living corners without saying a word. Just eye contact, they can hear the words without speaking them ~ momma saying if you need anything you know where to find me, and Aubrielle acknowledging momma's words and saying thank you with her return look.

Chapter 18

Aubrielle goes inside and take a long hot shower, which feels amazing. She does this every time she leaves the hospital. And like always after emerging from the shower she goes to Chances dresser to find one of his wife beaters to put on, and a pair of his boxers. But the dresser is empty. She runs over to the closet and sees all his work stuff is gone too. "What the fuck!" she screams. As she reaches for the house phone, she calls Blue on speaker phone and explains what just happen, and that she needs to know where he is. Blue finally tells her about the note and the key on the counter. "Blue, please tell me. where can I find him?" she pleads. Blue gives in and tells her. Brie gets dressed quickly and run over there. She pulls up at the lot and starts to feel panicky as not to know what to expect. what if he is aggressive again? what if he has a girl over her mind begins to race.

There are 3 steps going up to the apartment and a small window to the right of the door, she goes as quietly as she can to look in it, Chance is laying on the bed. No one else is there. But there is empty bottle of liquor everywhere, she stops counting at 10. She slowly and quietly turns the knob to see if it is open, he is laying on his stomach faces the other way, so chance doesn't see or hear it and she manages to get in the apartment. She closes the door as quietly as she can, slips off her flip flops so not to make a sound. Chance is snoring loudly, but she doesn't want to wake him. She climbs into bed with him and hugs him as tight as she can, she scares the shit out of Chance, and he flies over to see who is there and catches Aubrielle in the eye with his elbow. She screams in pain and pulls away while she tries to get up, but Chance is pulling her back to him.

"Brie, what the hell, I'm so sorry I didn't know it was you. I felt something turned around I didn't mean it. Please don't go." He says begging her. She stops fighting him and stays in his arms. She missed him so much.

She pulls away after a few minutes, Chance can she her eye is already turning black and blue. He jumps up to get her ice. He puts it on the side of her eye, they sit there in silence with their eyes locked on each other, not making a sound, yet it is as if they are speaking to each other.

"Why?" she finally asks him, she desperately needs to know why he left her.

"Nothing good can ever come from this this. We are two different, and now we must think of our beautiful babies. Brie I love you with everything I have in me but for me to really love you the way you deserve I need to let you go. So, you can be ok, and happy again, and be the mother our kids deserve. You all deserve better than me. I can't give you what you want or need." He explains slowly, as he tries to pick out every word carefully one by one. To make her understand that he is the problem, but of course she doesn't see it that way. As the tears plunge down her cheeks, chance wipes them away.

"I can't live my life without you Chance, you are the air I breathe. "she whispers. Chance not only sees in the moment she is never letting go, but for the first time in his life he felt all the love behind those words. He kisses her, she kisses him back, and of course pushes for more than just the kiss.

"No, Aubrielle. We can't have sex, the doctor said you needed to wait at least six weeks." He says pushing her away, annoyed she lets him go to make him think she is compiling. However, she waits until he falls asleep, she grabs two of his ties and ties him to the bed frame. She starts to undo his clothing, as she kisses his body. Chance finally wakes up to see what was going on. Aubrielle got him naked and standing at full attention. "You know this is not fair, right?" Chance said as he laughed, she couldn't help but also laugh. She was glad to see that he was in to and not mad because she wasn't following doctor's orders. "you can tie me up next, so you can have your turn with me." She says playfully demanding. She saddles up on Chance and rides him like this was the ride of her life, until they both cum. Chance tells her to let him go and then lay down on the bed on her stomach. Not saying a word, she does as she is told, fixing her ponytail along the way. Chance ties her hand to the headboard, face down. Then takes two more ties and ties her ankle to her wrist, fully exposing the middle of her he is about to work and is going to work all of it. For shits and giggles he grabs on more tie and blindfolds her. Aubrielle is beyond excited; the thought of him touching her and not knowing where when how or with what he will use is driving her crazy with excitement and anticipation. Chance begins by rubbing baby oil all over her body, he gives the buildup of her needing him some more time, as he continues to rub, she begs him to slide through it, but he isn't listening to her. He massages every inch of her down to her feet, before coating her toes in oil he begins to suck on her toes, driving Aubrielle over the edge, now screaming for him to take her, but instead of listening chance grabs another tie and gags her. After the knot is formed, Chance moves in position, He inserts his dick, and moves it in an out a few times quickly, she is feeling every bit of it, but Chance is really doing it to just get wet. After he feel like it is wet enough in one quick move he switches to anal sex. Aubrielle is so lost in the moment she doesn't even care, after the initial shock wears off, she helps him with his thoughts, by throwing her ass in the air after each stroke he gives her. Aubrielle takes over the motion of the thoughts, so Chance just sticks he dick out as far as he can and lets her ride it this way, until they reach the pinnacle point of their love making.

After they finish, he unties her. The both begin to think how they have the best sex after a huge fight, Aubrielle goes into the showers, Chances follows her. They get washed up and help each other as they keep making eye contact. Chance and Aubrielle have this weird connection, that even in silence they have the deepest of conversations. The peaceful feeling Aubrielle first felt when she got there is slowly slipping away and she starts to feel her anxiety start to build again, she looks over at Chance, who throws her a towel and tells her to be quiet just by putting his pointer finger up to his mouth. She sees panic in his eyes and starts to shake. Chance shuts the water off. Allowing the voice's, they both heard become clearer from the other side of the door.

"yea, looks like he is in the shower, and has a chick here too." The one man says

"Well, you got your orders ~ kill him. Torch this bitch, and make sure it burns to the ground." Another voice says. Chances looks at Brie, she is crying as obviously she hear the conversation too. Paralyzed she can't move, but Chance moves quickly and pulls clothes off the floor he had in the bathroom, he dress both himself and Aubrielle as fast has he can move and then turns the water on to get the clothing wet. He is preparing them to go through the flames. He grabs two towels and wets them before putting them over their heads. He pulls Brie's arms around his stomach. "Just put your head down and walk with me, do not let go." Chance says with fear in his voice, she nods to let him know she heard him, as she stares at flames now coming through the bottom of the door. Chance opens the door and begins to make their way through the fire, the smoke is thick but being sucked more out the front door that the 2 men left open then in room, and the windows that are now broken. The flames are huge and extremely hot, thank God, the apartment is small, "we are almost there" he screams over the crackling of the fire. They get to the doorway and the fire trucks are pulling up, just as a support beam from the ceiling breaks off and hits Aubrielle sending her back in the inferno. Chance goes to run back in the building to get her when the fireman pulls him out of the way and tosses him to the side and runs in and to grab Brie, he pulls her to safety. She is alive but is covered in burns. The EMT Crew rush her into the ambulance to get her to the hospital as quickly as they can.

Chapter 19

Chance is left at the scene; he falls to his knees in disbelief of what has happen. They notified Dexter of the fire on the lot and he called Javier, and NY 'Aire so the news is spreading as quick as the fire had.

Javier gets to the lot first, and goes running over to Chance, but the cops won't let anyone near him yet. They are about to question him, but before they do, they want to review the videotapes of the lot. E.M.T.'s is also still looking over him for any injuries, or burns he got during the incident.

Dexter finally arrives at the lot, and leads the officers over to the office, when they go into the building they see that all the back windows were smashed in and the DVR that records the video is missing, but ADT, gets the footage directly, so the cops call the for assistant. Shortly after they watch the footage to get an idea of what happen, to question him better.

"Mr. Curtis, we would like to question you." Detective Reyes says.

"How is Aubrielle?" he asks, no one is telling him anything.

"We are told she is stable but critical" the Detective said sadly. "please tell us what happen?" he continued.

Chance tells them what he knows which Is not much, just that they heard voices and the details of the conversation and then the fire. The detective asks Chance to review the tapes to see if he recognizes and of the men. Chance is in Shock when he sees the tapes and see lucky with one of Izzy's boys. Alexander "Lex" Allen. Chance tells the cops who the two men are, just as Demetrius and Angelina walk into the room. He sees Angelina out of the corner of his eye and that old grandmother look of disapproval he always gets from her, when she sees Chances has burns all over him too, she can't help but feel bad as he continues the story.

"why was Aubrielle behind you, and not in front of you the detective continued his integration.

"I put the wet clothes on us to protect us from the flames, I made her grab my waist to lead her out of the building and told her to keep her down. I thought I could protect her. I'm obviously much taller than she is, every time she saw a flame she became paralyzed and would not move, so I thought if she couldn't see in front of her and just moved on foot at a time that it would be easier on her. Plus, if anything was to fall or if they came back my whole body protected her. It worked until we got to the door. I told her we were almost there and stepped on to the step outside and she looked out from the under the towel and saw something and froze again and that's when the beam fell. I tried to pull her, but it didn't work." Chance said with the disbelief all over his voice. "I never meant for her be hurt in any way Angelina, you have to believe me. I love her. I even broke up with her tonight and told her to stay away from me because every time I try to do the right thing and protect her, she just gets hurt even more and each time it is worse. Ang- I'm SOOO sorry." Chances says sobbing as he turns his attention to her and forgets there is even detectives in the room, or Demetrius. Angelina hugs Chance, she knows everything he is saying is the truth but really wishes they would leave each other alone before one of them dies, as she prays it is not her sister. or Chance. She does like him as a person but knows that he is toxic, and it may not be his fault but that doesn't lessen how dangerous he is. "Can we please take him to the hospital now, he is not going anywhere, his girl and newborn babies are here and the rest of his family." Angelina vouches for him. Detective Reyes Shakes his head yes.

When they arrive at the hospital everyone is there, both sides of the families. Chances has tunnel vision he is just looking for Aubrielle, but the doctors are still evaluating her, and coming up with a treatment, and getting her comfortable to the best of their ability.

Chances goes to the next best thing, his babies. He is happy to see them doing well. Destiny is there, and quick to fill Chance in that Joanna has had a good night, and then looks at Chance and asks him what happen. He tells her the quick version and asked her if she can get an update on Aubrielle for him. Which she can look up in the computer and does it right away for him and now she is afraid for her friend and wants to know was much as he does. She learns that Aubrielle has 2nd degree burn on less than 50% of her body, and although very painful, if she can avoid any infections, she will be ok she explains to Chance as she reads the report.

Chances goes and sits with the babies, exhaustion has taken a hold of him, and this feeling a defeat is overbearing, he sinks into a deep depression, when out of nowhere Marcus runs over to him and punches him the face, Chance wasn't expecting it. He stumbled across the room trying to regain his balance when he knocked into one of the incubators, that Joanna s resting in. Destiny screams at them for them to stop and calls security to remove Marcus. "If she dies I will fucken kill you, you low- life piece of shit." He screams at Chances, as 4 guards wrestle him off the floor. Destiny brings Chance a clean towel, and some ice. Marcus did a good number on Changes face; she is surprised his jaw is still intact.

Ginamarie Foceri

He asked her to be alone with his children and not to let anyone in the room. He is overwhelmed with emotion. He cries, and prays, he is lost and doesn't know what to do, he has lost all hope, and can't bear the thought of going on without Aubrielle or worse yet. with her.

136

Chapter 20

It has been almost three months since the fire. Aubrielle and the babies are still in the hospital however, they will be discharged today. Chance is nervous not sure what to do, or what will happen. He has been making his presence at the hospital checking on his family clear but keeping his distance from Aubrielle despite her pleas for him.

Chance is still working at the lot; he was surprised Dexter didn't terminate him for being such a liability. They found Lucky and arrested him on an unrelated charge, although the investigation is still pending. Lex has been laying low, but the police are still looking for him. Chance has also been laying low, of sorts he really hasn't left the hospital at all, other than to work when they really need someone, or he needs money for the bills.

Today, after work he goes by the house to start the preparations for his family's home coming. Momma Shaw as done her best to clean it, but Chance gets a cleaning service to come in a do a deep cleaning since Aubrielle and the babies are still fragile and need to avoid infections. He has them clean every area of the house top to bottom, even doing all the bedding. He waits at the house for the 5 hours they are there when his cell starts to blow up.

Shavon has been calling him none stop today, and he knows he should answer it because she is due at any time, but he doesn't care. He just wants his family and Aubrielle to be happy and healthy. The cleaning crew has gone, he has showered and changed and is on his way back up to the hospital.

Chance puts the car in park, in the garage at the hospital and as he prepares to step out of the car, he sees Shavon in the rear view. He exhales as hard as he can, and mentally prepares himself for this fight.

"So, I gave you your space to deal with your little issue and you haven't called to check on your other family in months, you know I am due anytime now, right? And we need to figure this out." Shavon screams. Chance shakes his no, "There is nothing to figure out, I meet with a lawyer I am signing over my parental rights, I refuse to be a part of your scheme, you used me and trick me to get pregnant I want nothing to do with you or that baby." Chance snaps back. He feels terrible for the kid and doesn't want his child growing up like that, but he feels he has no choice in the matter. "Or the only other option is, I'm coming for my kid – but either way there is no you and me – no family – no co-parenting no nothing!!!!" As they are talking Chance see Detective Reyes and Santiago pull in. the parking lot. "Besides, I am no good, look at all the shit that has happened to Brie since we have been together. Shavon if you were a real mother you would take this opportunity and run away from me to protect you and your baby, not look for a pay out." He says sadly, seeing the detectives reminds him of why he is at the hospital.

"So, because I want my children to know their father, I am a bitch and a poor mother, but I doesn't see Aubrielle running away from you and you still think she is a saint, really what the fuck. Could you be any more of a hypocrite?" She fires.

"I have told Brie the same thing, she is as thick headed as you are. I'm toxic, you need to stay away from ~ no one else can get hurt behind me and my past. "Chance says with a glimpse of his regret and depression all over his voice. But she is to vain to notice anything but herself.

Chance sees another car coming into the parking lot, his heart sinks and he doesn't know why he all the sudden got a bad feeling. "I got to go, be safe. Let me know when you deliver." Chance says as he starts to walk off. He goes in the opposite direction of where Shavon is standing. But like the dumbass she is she follows him. "Chance I am not done with you." She screams.

The black hummer, that chance saw coming in has stopped and is watching them.

Inside the hummer is Lex, and Izzy. "what do you want to do Izzy? There he is, I think that is his girl." Lex questions.

"is it, I thought she had the babies?" Izzy says.

"Man, I'm not sure, he has his main joint and his side one – they were both knocked out at the same time." Lex replies. Then continues "and the way she is coming at him she is one of them, and those are his kids."

"You are carrying Lex?" Izzy's asks him.

"And you know this" Lex sings to him.

"Get ready." Izzy directs.

The car starts to move again, Chance tells Shavon to start walking in the other direction, he thinks this truck is about to do something, but again in her hardheaded ways she thinks he is trying to get rid of her, Chance is walking away, back up through a row of cars, and she is right in front of him.

"You are going around to the other row to get him in the line of fire?" Lex asks.

"Nope, go for the bitch first. "he says like the coldhearted mother fucker he is. "He took my mother. So, I am taking everyone in his life." He finishes with.

The hummer drives down the lane and opens fire on Shavon and Chance. Chances tries to push Shavon out of the path of the bullets, but it does now good, she is hit 3 times. Out of nowhere Detective Reyes and Santiago appear shooting back at the hummer; and kill both men inside, then call the hospital from them to bring a gurney and get Shavon in the Operating Room immediately. Chance is trying to stop the blood from pouring out of her, he hated this bitch for what she did, but didn't want this to happen to her or anyone and not to the baby. He did have love for the baby but in a weird way and not like his children who laid peacefully in the hospital. He knew it was because his feeling for their mother were completely different than his feelings for Aubrielle.

"Chance, please don't let anything happen to the babies. If it is a matter of my life or theirs – choice theirs." She cried.

"Don't talk Shavon save your strength, they are coming you're going to be ok. You have to be." Chance says with tears in his eyes.

"No, I'm not going to make it, please promise me Chance. I'm so sorry don't hate them for what I did – they are innocent in this – please promise me." She begs, he nods in agreement. And whispers "shhh, rest up."

Detective Reyes and Santiago are right there, helping Chance Apply pressure, when the hospital staff comes for her, by this time there is other police units on the scene, and they begin to process everything that just went down.

Chapter 21

They rush Shavon into surgery to try and save her and the babies. The detectives let Chance go to Aubrielle and his children, he is in shock and they know he is not going anywhere. The hospital is on lock down though, no one else can enter or exit it until the scene is processed. Chance is pacing in the hallway he doesn't want to tell Aubrielle that he was just in a drive by and her ex- best friend and mother of her other children is dying as we speak. Chance mind starts to race. "Children". "why did Shavon keep using that word like there was more than one baby?" the keeps thinking repeatedly. Aubrielle comes from around the corner smiling from ear to ear, she is delighted to see him. (They have been around each other and have conversations about the babies and other that it's been meaning conversation and never about that night or the status of their relationship. She asks like everything is normal and she tries to avoid her most importantly more pain. But he knows she still hasn't given up on him, so neither has he.) Her smile always takes him away from this world and his problems. She then notices chance has blood on his shirt. "Oh my God what happen? You ok?" she says reaching for his shirt, to show him he has blood on it.

"Yes, I am ok, but we need to talk." Chance says with a blank look on his face. Aubrielle is nervous she can't read him and has no idea what he is about to tell her.

"Baby come over and sit with me for a minute. "Chance says grabbing her hand and leading her over to a waiting area in the hospital.

Dr. Mandina comes around the corner. Chances heart sinks and tell Aubrielle to hold on a second and not to leave this spot. "Baby, please just wait right here. I promise, I will tell you everything in detail just give me a minute." he says. She shakes her head in agreement.

"Hi Doc, I guess you have an update." Chances looking worried.

"I'm do. Shavon didn't make it but the babies are stable." Dr. Mandina says. "Babies" Chance asks. "Yes, you have a son and a daughter." Dr. Mandina says. She gives Chance a hug. "I know she wasn't the best person and tricked you into this. I'm sure it is really confusing for you." She continued. Chance shook he head yes, well looking at the floor."

Chance makes his way back to Aubrielle. She sees the sadness and confusion in his eyes, she knows this is serious. "you ok, baby?' she asks as he sits down on the couch next to her.

"I am but a lot happened today, and I don't know how to tell you." He confuses. "Chance really at this point you can tell me anything we have been through it all pretty much, we have face everything except the situation with Shavon and the baby." Aubrielle replies.

"No really, we never spoke about the here and now, the aftermath of the fire. Or what now either." He says

She looks at him confused. "I love you; this was not your fault what more is there to talk about." She says

"A lot, it's kind of is. The story about the fire has to do with my mother's murder." Chance begins, he tells her all about his childhood friend Izzy, Izzy's mother, her drug and prostitution issue and her suicide. The broken arm and how Izzy blamed him for it all. "Brie, I didn't know any of this when I met you, it was until after I met Demetrius he found me after one of our fights, I went back to the marina where I took you on our first date, and he came up on me and told me what that bullshit was about that night you found out you were pregnant, when we were at your mom's." He tells her and continues the story "I need a few days to process what I heard – my boy killed my mother on some revenge shit that was bullshit. That fucked me up, when I had a minute to let marinate, I was coming home to tell you and Shavon showed up with this bull shit about her being pregnant."

"Have you heard from her, I'm sure she is due at any moment." Brie asked curiously to see how much commination these two had.

"today was the first time in months, I think the last time was the day of the DNA test, but today was the last time, she had the babies today, a boy and a girl. But today will be our last conversation. "he says with a real sadness on his face. "Miss her already?" Brie barks

"No Brie – Dam. I'm trying to tell you Shavon is dead, she died today." He says

Aubrielle looks shocked, she hated her alright but never wished this on her, well really those babies and her parents.

"during delivery? Did you use the babies yet, a boy and a girl I can't believe she had twins too" She asks him?

"No to both questions. "Chance says, still looking for a way to tell her. "Well, let's go" Brie said.

"Where?" he asked

"To see your babies" she replies

"not yet, I have more to tell you. I don't know how to – so I'm just going to run with it. you heard the hospital was on a lock down, right?" he asks her, she nods and says, "yea something happen in the garage, but the hospital downplayed it like it was nothing." She said.

"this afternoon, when I get here, Shavon was waiting for me in the parking lot she was demanding to know what my intentions were with the babies. I told her that it was either to sign my rights away or take them away because I wasn't raising a family with her. And that she was stupid because she should run away from me, I'm toxic." He sadly tells her.

"Chance, where is this going" She asks him

"We were talking, and I see a car pull in the lot, its Detective Reyes and Santiago. I tell her to leave, she is going back and forth with me about this whole thing with the babies and another car pulls in – I tell her to go the other way after the hummer stops and is watching us. I got a bad feeling but she of course didn't listen she just followed me, I started to walk away from her to get away from her, from the conversation and because I had a bad feeling like the night of the fire, the truck started to move and this time it opened fire at us, I tried to push her out of the way but she has hit 3 times, and then the detective show up, out of nowhere, and shot and killed Izzy and Lex. I applied pressure to her wounds until help came and they rushed her into the operating room, where they lost her, but saved the babies. She begged me in her last breath, her last words not to hate them and to take care of the babies because she knew she wasn't going to make it. I was looking at her and all I kept thinking was thank God it was her and not you. I'm so sorry Brie, another lost to you made by me. I'm a really bastard, I couldn't even think of her or those babies ~ I could only think of You, Jonna, and Antonio." He says with tears coming down his face.

Aubrielle wipes away his tears and says "if you're a bastard then I am a bitch, because I can't help but think of the same thing, I loved Shavon for many years but really she never had my best interest at heart. She meant to hurt me, she was never there for me, was never a real friend to me. I was always the friend to her, the one who was there for her, the one who cleaned up her mess, that was our roles. And I will continue that by helping you raise our children together." She takes Chances by the hands without saying another word and leads him the nursery to meet his babies for the first time. This moment was precious to her, as this did right at least one wrong Shavon did to her. Shavon stole the moment Chance and her would meet their babies together for the first time like she had dreamed. She robbed them of that moment but gave it back to them just now by let her be with Chance to meet these babies.

Shavon's mother, Nina Stephanie, as she was named after both of her grandmothers as well, but everyone called her Stephanie, is in the nursery when they get there, Aubrielle and Chance were both very surprised that she wasn't a mess. She gave Aubrielle a huge hug, and Chance too. They all extend their sorry to each other, first her mother to Chance for all the evil her daughter caused, and then Chance for her daughter's death. "you didn't kill her Chance do not burden yourself with that, that was karma. She had no business pregnant or here harassing you the way she did." Stephanie said. "do you guys have names picked out for your two new additions?" she asked them point to Shavon's babies. Aubrielle and Chance looked at each other confused, not about the names but the fact that they thought that Stephanie would want custody. "I am to old, and clearly I wasn't a good mother, or my daughter would have not been so set on hurting everyone, the way she did. I want you guys to raise these babies, along with Antonio and Joanna. I know you're are going to be a fabulous mother Aubrielle, your huge heart is always so pure and fill of love. Chance, this is a clean start for you. All your demons are dead, and the love you have for your family and Aubrielle should be applauded. Take this fresh start and never look back. You will never get anywhere, if you are always looking in the rearview mirror. Promise me that and promise me you will give me the chance to be a better grandmother then I was a mother." Stephanie says her eyes filled with tears of love as she holds the babies together. Aubrielle and Chance nod in agreement as they hug each other. They both had not had the time to think about what Stephanie said and how profound this moment really was, this moment of new beginnings, new life, new chapters to fill the pages with and the love that filled this one room. Aubrielle and Chances families have now joined them after hearing the news, and the hospital finally lifting the lockdown. With Adrianna is holding Joanna, and momma Shaw is hold James. Everyone is there to meet the new additions.

"I got it" Chance yells, "Arianna Stephanie Shaw Curtis to keep in line with the intimal them and grandmothers, and Josiah James Shaw Curtis for other boy, both my boys after me with their middle names and keeping in line again with the intimal theme as well"

Everyone agrees.

Chapter 22

A few days pass since Arianna and Josiah were born and are being discharged today, Aubrielle, Joanna and Antonio were already released. Getting ready to leave the hospital Chance and Aubrielle lock their 4 babies car seats inside their new minivan, Chance got from the lot. Chance helps Aubrielle into the car and pass her the seat belt before closing the door. Chance gets into the van on the driver's side and becomes overwhelmed with emotion as he looks back at his babies, remembering what Stephanie said he turns around and looks at his babies, but not through the rearview mirror.

After starting to car to make their journey home, Chance pops in his favorite Mixtape. ON THE BRINK OF GREATNESS BY M.i. Nyce and Bigface Bennie, to one of his favorites his songs, Ride or Die ft. Dex.

"you know, you're still my blind spot?" He asks Aubrielle. "I'll take my dance with you." She says with a giggle, as they always quote their favorite lyrics from the song.

As they head down, the road hand in hand looking only out at their bright new start, to this beautiful unwritten chapter, the look at one another, and repeat in unison the last line to their favorite song, and first line of their new chapter "All I need is you."

Printed in the United States
By Bookmasters